... III in a series
"Narrow Gauge Railways of Europe"

FORTRESS RAILWAYS
OF THE
BALTIC SHORES

by

Mehis Helme

Plateway Press

ISBN 1 871980 20 8

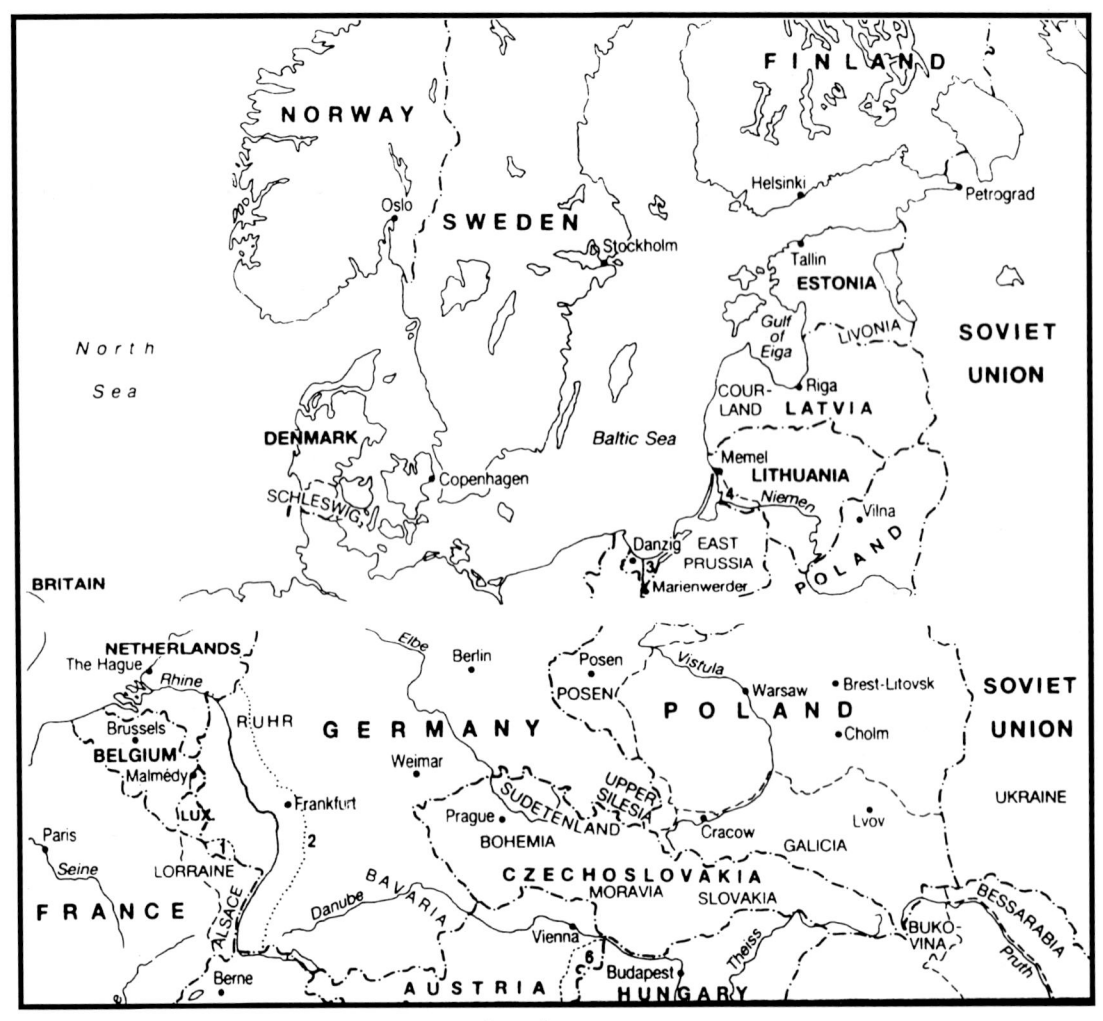

Location map

© Mehis Helme / Plateway Press 1994

All rights reserved. No part of this publication may be reproduced, stored in a retrieval system, or transmitted, in any form or by any means, electronic, mechanical, photocopying, recording or otherwise, without the prior written permission of the publisher.

Printed in Great Britain by Wayzgoose PLC, East Road, Sleaford, Lincs.

ISBN 1 871980 20 8

Cover artwork by John Holroyd

Typesetting by Martin Snow, Intersoft Multimedia

Book design by Keith Taylorson

Front cover illustrations:
(Upper) delivered to the Tallin Fortress railway only weeks before the outbreak of World War 1, Orenstein & Koppel 0-10-0 No. 7208/14 is pictured in the post-war years.
(Lower) a mixed train at Kuressaare, on the 60cm gauge "Feldbahn" railway built by the German Army, in 1924

CONTENTS

		Page
	Introduction	5
Chapter 1	The "Peter the Great Naval Fortress"	7
Chapter 2	The Forward Position and its Railway Network	9
Chapter 3	Strategic Islands and their Railways	11
Chapter 4	The Tallinn Naval Fortress - Coastal Defences	13
Chapter 5	The Tallinn Naval Fortress - Land Defences	17
Chapter 6	Railways of the Tallinn Naval Fortress	23
Chapter 7	Locomotives and Rolling Stock	29
Chapter 8	The Railways under German Occupation (1918-1919)	35
Chapter 9	War of Independence - and after	39
Chapter 10	Nationalisation of the Narrow Gauge Railways	47
Chapter 11	Later History of the Fortress Locomotives	55
Chapter 12	The Railways under German Occupation (1941-44)	59
Chapter 13	The Railways under Soviet Control	61
Chapter 14	Relics of the Naval Fortress Railways	69
	Bibliography	71
Appendix 1	Orenstein and Koppel locomotives delivered to the Fortress Railways	71
Appendix 2	French-built Russian field railway M series locomotives	72
Appendix 3	Russian 86 series field railway steam locomotives	73
Appendix 4	German "Feldbahn" locomotives in Estonia	73
	Table of Locomotive Dimensions	74

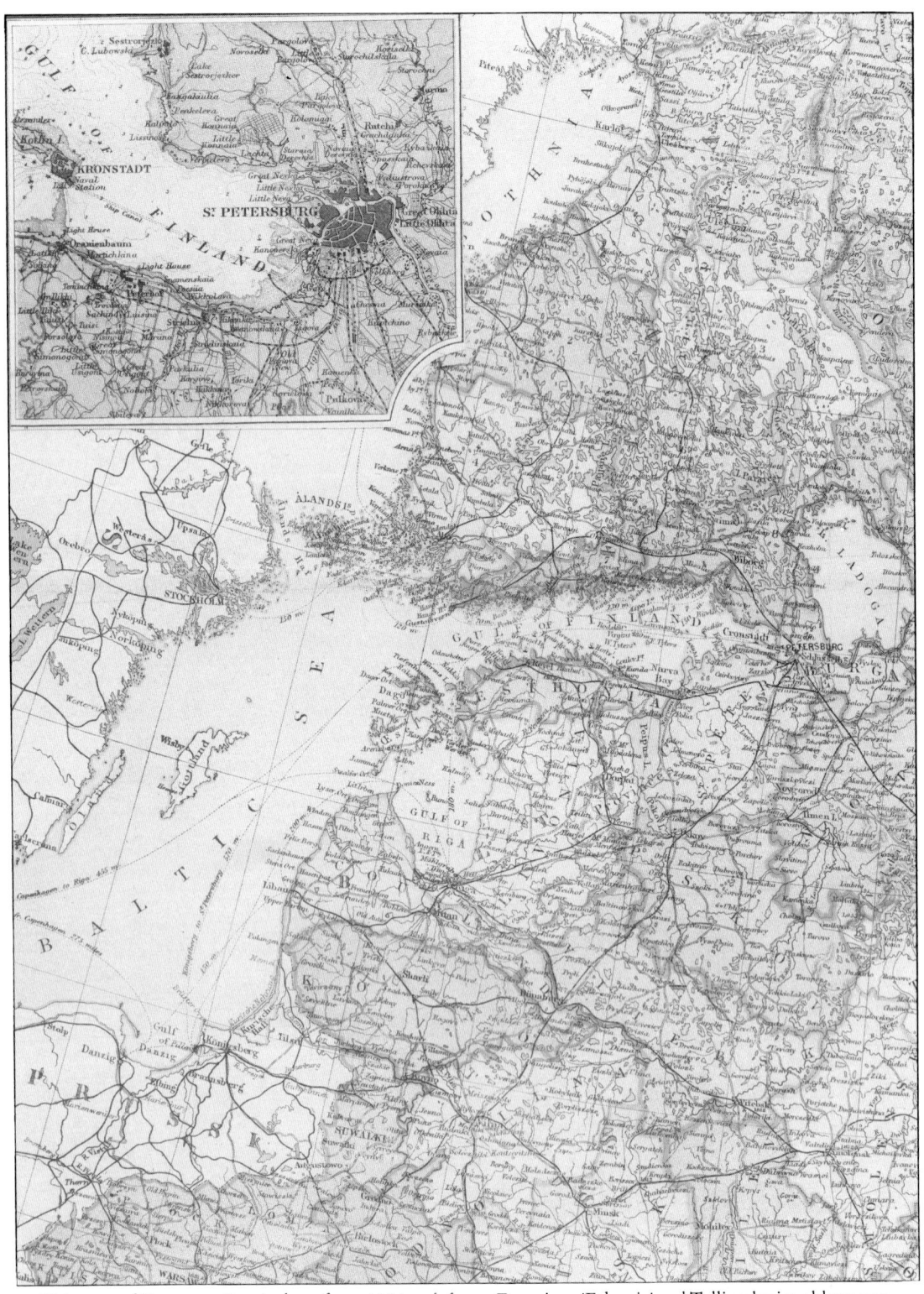

This map of European Russia dates from 1894 and shows Estonia as 'Ethonia' and Tallinn by its older name, Revel. (Inset): St. Petersburg and the Kronstadt naval base.

(Plateway Press)

INTRODUCTION

The republic of Estonia lies on the eastern shores of the Baltic sea. It is the northernmost of a group of countries known as the Baltic States, the others being Latvia and Lithuania. Estonia has been ruled at various times by Denmark, Sweden, Germany and Russia, whose first conquest of the country was in 1710. Industrialisation began in the l9th Century and soon Estonia was one of the most industrialised areas in the Russian Empire, including shipbuilding, metal and machinery industries. As the Century progressed, increasing prosperity fuelled a growing nationalism, but Czarist control ensured that Russia kept a firm grip on Estonia's affairs, as it occupied a pivotal strategic position protecting Russia's Baltic shores.

It was in the wake of the Russian defeat at the hands of the Japanese in 1905 that massive fortification works were put in hand along the Estonian coast and on the offshore approaches to St Petersburg, Russia's principal naval base, stimulating the development of a network of narrow gauge railways which is described in detail in the following pages.

Wider events were to shape the fate of the fortresses, and the railways that served them. On 7 November 1917 the Bolsheviks seized power in Petrograd (as St Petersburg had been renamed), sparking off the Civil War destined to rage for almost three years. Peace negotiations held at Brest-Livosk between the Bolsheviks and a still undefeated Germany broke down, and on 18 February 1918 German forces advanced into areas of Russia, including Estonia, giving the fortresses their first chance to fire shots in anger. Other fortifications were demolished by the retreating Russian armies, but the railways survived and were put to use by the German occupying forces, who also constructed new 60cm gauge "Feldbahn" railways of their own. Two years of sporadic warfare against both the Russians and the Germans were necessary before the Tartu Peace Treaty of 2 February 1920 was concluded, and Estonia recognised as a sovereign state.

Independence was to last a mere 20 years. Under the Hitler-Stalin pact of 1939, Estonia became part of the Soviet sphere of influence. The country was occupied by Soviet forces in 1940 and a pro-Russian Government installed. Then, following the Nazi invasion of Russia, German troops occupied areas of Estonia from July 1941: once again the fortress railways found themselves back in the front line. When the tide of war turned, the Germans retreated and by November 1944 Estonia was back under Soviet domination, an era destined to last a further 45 years until the country's long awaited achievement of independence in the wake of the collapse of Soviet communism in the late 1980's.

The history of the republic's fortification railways through ninety years of turmoil, revolution, counter revolution, uneasy peace, and war has been pieced together by Estonian researcher Mehis Helme, and is recounted in detail in the pages that follow. However the story of the fortress railways did not end in 1945. Some military lines were absorbed into the Estonian State Railways and one at least retained a public passenger service until 1962. Even more remarkably, some sections of railway remain in being, under the control of the Russian military, even now. It is possible that in the new economic climate that some surviving remains may be preserved and even developed for leisure purposes, ensuring their survival, albeit in a changed role, into a second century.

ACKNOWLEDGMENTS

The publication of this work in the English language was instigated by an approach to the present publishers from Finnish enthusiast and writer Reino Kalliomaki. The work was translated by Mart Aru. Final editing was carried out by Keith Taylorson.

1. During the Russo-Japanese war of 1904-5, Czar Nicholas despatched Russia's Baltic Fleet to the Pacific. The Russian ships were intercepted in the Tsushima Strait by a Japanese force under Admiral Togo and all but four were destroyed - an event commemorated in this impressionistic Japanese propaganda picture. Russia's defeat by a 'barbarian' enemy sent shockwaves through Society and Government and led directly to the development of the Baltic Coast fortresses and the railways that served them.

(Plateway Press)

Chapter 1
The "Peter the Great Naval Fortress"

It was a time when the Russian Empire had recently emerged from two major wars, with Turkey (1877-1878) and with Japan (1904-1905). The last mentioned had taught a lesson to the generals of the imperial army, whose self-assurance had lulled their vigilance, leading them to underestimate the enemy. The result was crushing defeat both on land and on sea. It induced the Russians to think about the fortification of their capital, St. Petersburg, against a possible enemy attack. A number of committees were set up, some of them charged with the working out of a defence plan for the Gulf of Finland. However, the military headquarters, still geared to think in old, well-established patterns, would not listen to the opinions and suggestions tabled by the committees, despite the deplorable consequences of the last war. Accordingly, only minor repairs and alterations continued to be carried out at the Kronstadt naval base. Only in 1908 was it understood that modern defence works were also necessary westward of Kotlin island, on the south and north coasts of the Gulf of Finland. This is how the powerful Krasnaya Gorka and Ino batteries were born.

Working out a new state defence plan for the Russian empire started with the respective Czar's decree of 1907, calculated to be carried out in ten years. It put forward the completely new idea of establishing a set of coastal batteries on the Tallinn (Reval)—Porkkala (Borgå) line. The plan also envisaged the modernisation of weaponry at the existing positions at Kronstadt and Viborg. Tallinn was to be turned into the operational base of the Russian navy. The initial version of the plan suggested a major naval port in the Muuga Bay, but soon its location was altered in favour of Tallinn. It was thought all work there could be completed by 1916. However, it was only on 18 August 1909 that the Czar issued a decree on the financing of the project. The drawings for the Tallinn-Porkkala defence line were completed in 1911 and approved by the Czar on 16 November. According to the plans, the main idea of

2. Tallinn Bay on 29 June 1914, the day that Czar Nicholas II laid the foundation stone for the Naval Fortress in Tallinn.

the line was to guarantee and facilitate the operational activity of the Russian Navy in repulsing an attack by enemy naval forces, as well as action in case such a breakthrough was successful.

The hub of the system was Tallinn whose coastal batteries were to defend the naval port and warehouses under construction at Paljassaare and guarantee the free passage of warships into the Gulf of Finland. The fire power of the defence line was to be concentrated on the island of Naissaar (Nargen). The heavy western coastal batteries of Tallinn were also to cover the waters of Paldiski (Baltischport). This defence system was later given the name of *Emperor Peter the Great Naval Fortress*. Very soon, however, it became clear that the Tallinn—Porkkala and Kronstadt batteries were not enough to carry out an effective defence of St. Petersburg, for Tallinn could easily be taken by land. Another vulnerable point was the West-Estonian archipelago which an enemy could capture in order to establish naval bases there and continue warfare from them. The only sensible solution seemed to be to shift the defence lines farther out to the west. This gave birth to a gigantic defence plan which included the following positions: 1. Forward position: Tahkuna—Hanko 2. Muhu Strait position: from Sôrve to Kôpu peninsula 3. Main position: Tallinn—Porkkala 4. Flanging position: Islands and headlands off Helsinki 5. Reserve position: Meriküla—Rankkisaari 6. Kronstadt position: Krasnaya Gorka—Ino and Kotlin island 7. Åland position (see Map below). It was a system planned to guarantee the defence of St. Petersburg from the external enemy. On 26 April 1913 the Czar issued a solemn ukaze on the building of the naval fortress. It was divided into three main parts—the south and the north sectors and between them the sea secor. The south sector was stationed in Estonia, the north sector in Finland. Tallinn was appointed the centre of the fortress. The total cost of building over the next five-year period was established at 92.4 million roubles. That sum was later increased. The building work started in 1913. Transportation in the naval fortress area relied on cobble-stone highways and narrow-gauge railways.

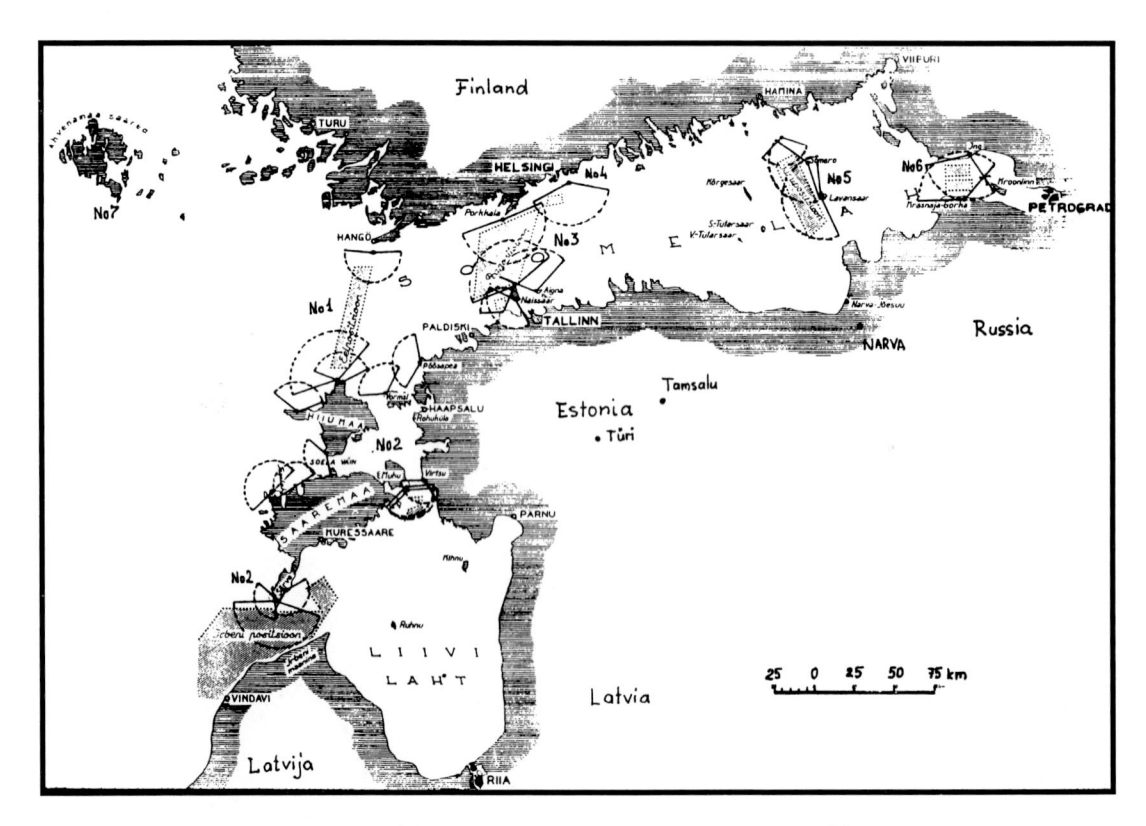

THE NAVAL FORTRESSES IN THE GULF OF FINLAND, THEIR POSITIONS AND FIRING SECTORS OF THE COASTAL BATTERIES.

Chapter 2
The Forward Position and its Railway Network

The forward position was stationed on the Tallinn—Hanko line. The southern wing of the position was made up of the Tahkuna and Lehtma batteries on Hiiumaa (Dago/ Dagö) island. The Tahkuna battery No 39 lies to the northeast of the village which is now destroyed. There were four 12-in guns on the position. An approximately 6 km stretch of 750 mm railway was built in 1914 from the position to Lehtma harbour. On its way to the harbour, 3.5 km down the route, the railway passed the Lehtma battery No 38 which was armed with four 6-in Canet guns. A shed for two locomotives was built at Tahkuna. The locos, built by the Orenstein & Koppel company of Germany, were 90 HP 0-6-0 tanks built in spring 1914. The 8-tonne flat wagons with bogies were all built by Artur Koppel of St. Petersburg in 1913. The northern wing of the forward position was situated to the southwest of the Hanko headland, a few miles from Russarö island. Three two-barrel batteries were set up there. The 9.2-in guns for it were ordered from the American Bethlehem Steel Company. From the north the rear was defended by a 7.5-in battery and two anti-aircraft batteries.

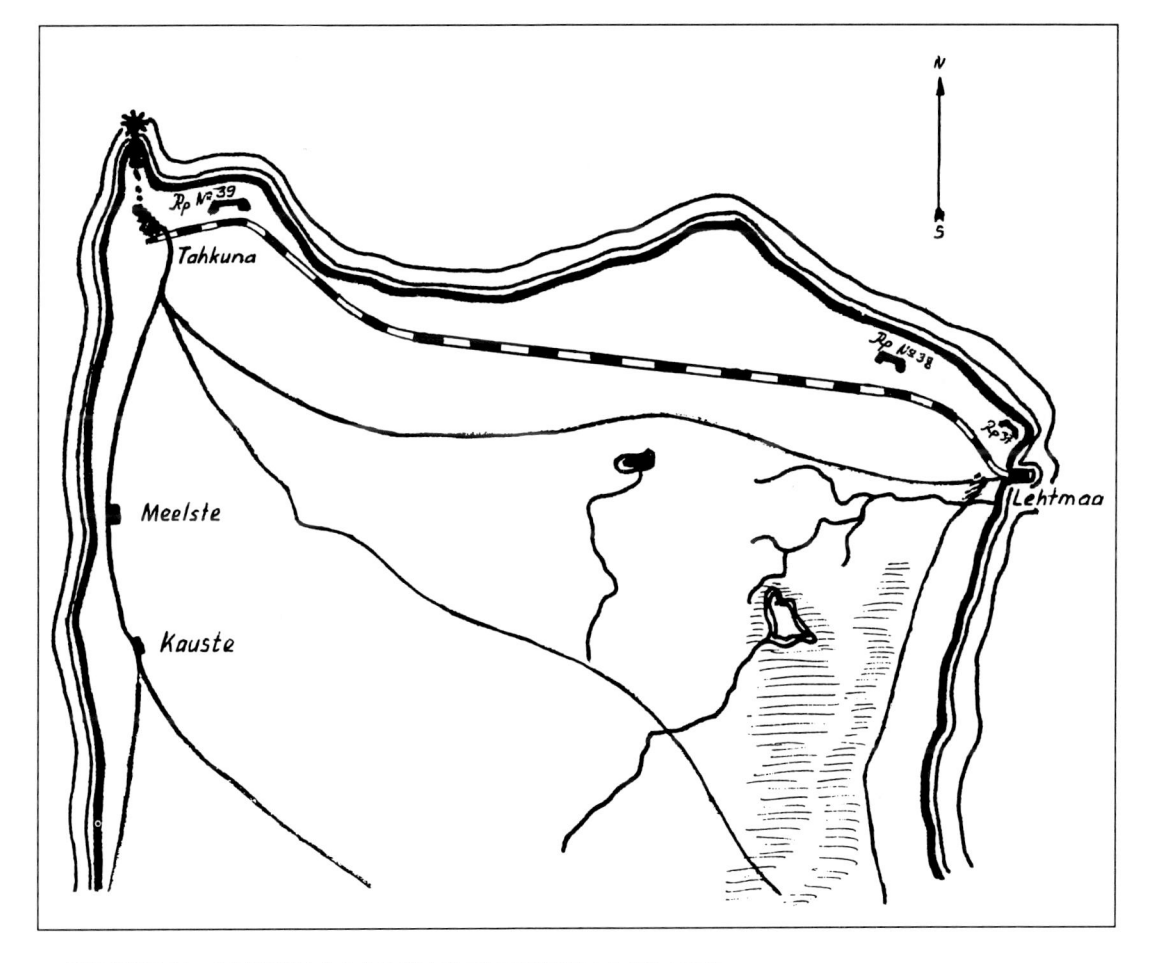

TAHKUNA - LEHTMAA RAILWAY ON HIIUMAA ISLAND

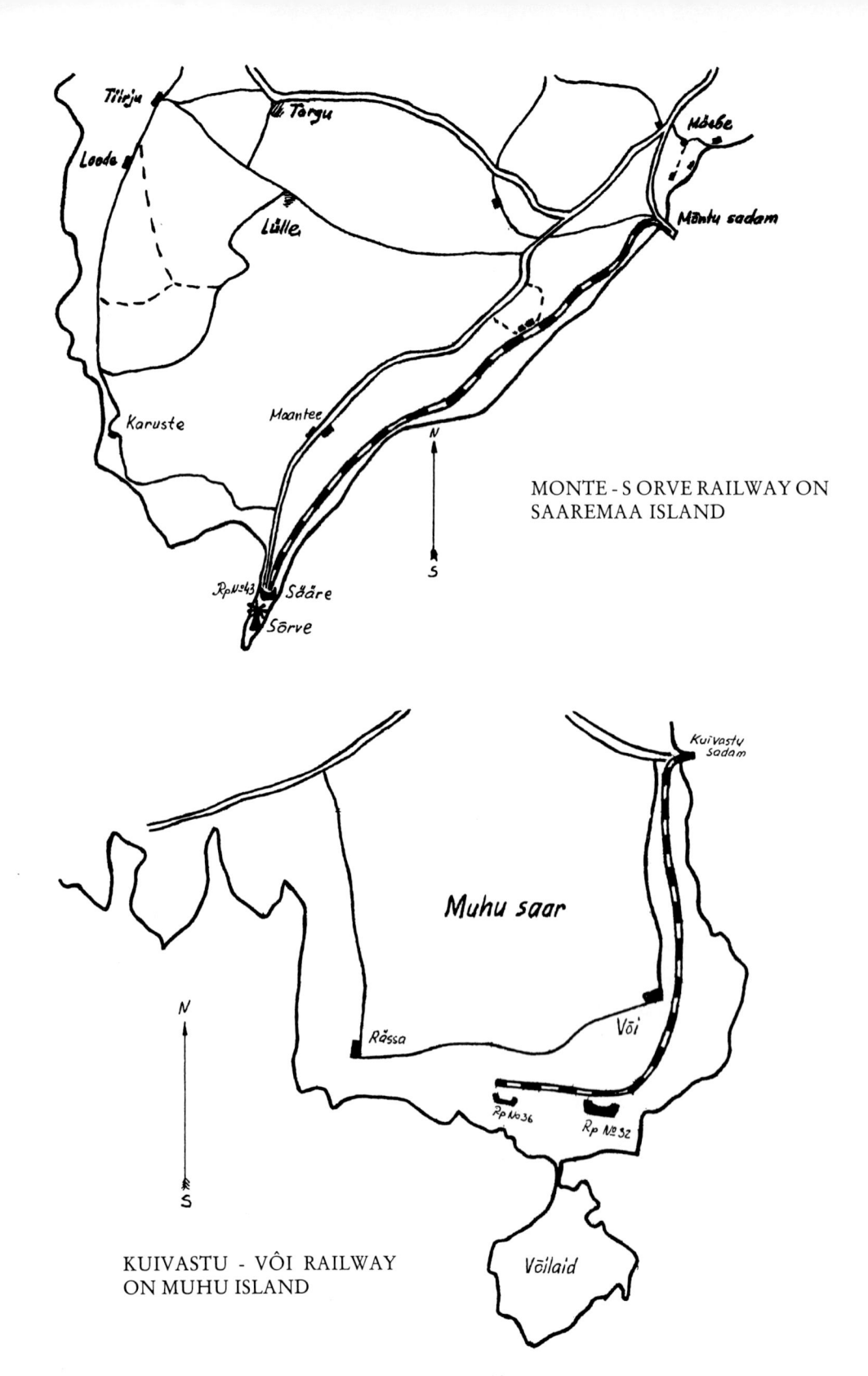

MONTE - SORVE RAILWAY ON
SAAREMAA ISLAND

KUIVASTU - VÕI RAILWAY
ON MUHU ISLAND

Chapter 3
Strategic Islands and their Railways

Muhu Strait Position and its rail network

The Muhu Strait (Moonsund) position occupied a much larger proportion of Estonian territory than the forward position. It extended from Hiiumaa island to Point Sôrve Säär and from Saaremaa (Oesel) island to the mainland via the islands of Muhu (Moon) and Vormsi (Worms). The main points on Hiiumaa were Sôru, Lehtma and Hirmuste; on Saaremaa Undva, Ninase, Loode, Murasti, Kihelkonna, Karuste, Mäebe and Sôrve-Sääre; on Muhu Vôi; on Vormsi the north coast, and on the mainland Rohuküla and Virtsu. Most of these positions were provided with 6-in Canet guns, but there were also bigger and smaller calibres. Narrow-gauge railways were laid out from Môntu harbour to Sôrve-Sääre, from Hirmuste harbour to the battery, from Kuivastu harbour to Vôi, on Vormsi island from the lighthouse to the battery. The building of a temporary narrow-gauge railway was started between Roomassaare harbour and Kuressaare, in order to improve the transport of building materials , but this project was never completed.

Môntu-Sôrve Line

A 4.5 km 750 mm railway was built at the southwestern tip of Saaremaa island from Môntu harbour to Sôrve-Sääre village where battery No 43 was situated, with two armoured turrets and four 12-in guns. One 90 HP 0-6-0 tank locomotive built at the Orenstein & Koppel works in Germany in 1914 was in use on the line. The 8-tonne flat wagons with bogies were 8-tonne built in 1913 at the Artur Koppel wagon plant in St. Petersburg.

Kuivastu-Vôi Line

In Muhu a 6 km stretch of 750-mm railway was built from Kuivastu harbour to batteries No 32 and 36 located about 1,250 to the west of Vôi village. The batteries were armed with five 10-in Durlacher and four 6-in Canet guns. Two 50 HP 0-6-0 tank locomotives built by the German O&K company in 1914 were taken into use on the line. The wagons in use were the same as at Môntu and Tahkuna.

3. A 10in gun of the Vôi battery on Muhu island.

Hirmuste Line

A narrow-gauge railway was built on Hiiumaa from Hirmuste harbour to battery No 47 located 500m from the shore near the Kôpu lighthouse. The battery was provided with four 6-in Canet guns. Transport on the railway line from Hirmuste harbour to the battery was by horse-drawn trolleys.

Vormsi Line

At the same time a stretch of railway a few km in length was built on the island of Vormsi. It led from the north coast harbour to the lighthouse where the warehouses were situated. The 750 mm railway serviced the north shore battery No 30 which was provided with four 6-in Canet guns. Also in Vormsi a steam engine was in use. It was the same type used on Muhu—built in 1914 by O&K of Germany. The wagons were of standard stock—similar to the ones used elsewhere at the Muhu Strait position.

Roomassaare-Kuressaare Line

In 1917, the Russian military started to build a narrow gauge railway from Roomassaare harbour to Kuressaare in order to improve the transportation of building materials for the fortification works. The end of the line was to be in the yard of Wildenberg's factory where the warehouses were situated. However, the work did not progress very far, because it was interrupted by the occupation of the island by German troops. The railway was to be 750 mm gauge and 3 km in length.

Åland Position

The building of the Åland position started after the World War broke out, in order to prevent the enemy from penetrating into the Gulf of Bothnia. Emplacements were built on ten islands around Åland, for a total of 37 guns. A railway was built on one of the islands. The locos were 0-4-0s built by O & K, and the flat wagons were 5...8 tonne capacity.

4. An unidentified locomotive which served the defence forces in the Åland islands.

Chapter 4
The Tallinn Naval Fortress - Coastal Defences

The land area intended to be expropriated for the Tallinn Naval Fortress was 1,169.5 dessiatines, and for the land front 2,592 dessiatines (1 dessiatine = 10,925 sq m). 99 dessiatines in the vicinity of the town was set aside for the fortress railway. The total area of land thus made up 3,868 dessiatines. Of the sums paid out for the expropriation of land to be taken under the naval fortress 61.9 per cent went to Naissaar islanders—638,755 roubles in all. The payment was by special order and included compensation for the loss of the main source of livelihood, sealing and fishing, by the peasants on Naissaar's state lands. Depending on the number of boats the total sum paid per family ranged from 750 to 1,500 roubles in gold. Aegna island peasants did not receive this compensation, because there the land was expropriated from the owner of the island, Felix von Schotländer, the landlord of Viimsi. In August 1914 it appeared that Russian industry was not capable of providing the country's navy with the necessary weapons, ammunition and armoured plate. Immediately the supply of the Peter the Great Naval Fortress was ranked only as third priority. By various machinations, however, it was possible to improve the situation a little. The south sector of the naval fortress, i.e. its part lying in Estonia, was divided into two: a) the 7-verst zone comprising the communes of Keila, Harku, Saue, Kurna, Nehatu (with Aegna island), Naissaar, Prangli (with Aksi island), part of the communes of Padise (with the Pakri peninsula), Raasiku and Jõelähtme. The islands it comprised were Aegna, Naissaar, Prangli, Aksi, Kräsuli, Kumbli, Pandju and the two Paljassaar islands. b) the 20-verst zone comprising the communes of Pakri, Padise, Keila, Laitse, Harku, Kirna-Kohatu, Saue, Kohila, Kurna, Nehatu, Rae, Kose-Uuemõisa, Jõelähtme, Raasiku, Peningi, Kiiu, Anija, Naissaare and Prangli.

The Sea Front

The coastal defences consisting of the batteries in the vicinity of and on the islands and headlands off Tallinn, as well as the headquarters, railway systems, communication sites, warehouses etc. were called the sea front of the fortress. It comprised Naissaar island, Suurupi, Kakumäe, Aegna island, Viimsi, Paljassaare, Prangli island, Aksi island, Pakri island and warehouses at Mustamäe. The first detailed plans for the sea front were completed in 1912. It had three main centres of gravity: a) at Naissaar a 14-in battery (three double-barrelled armoured turrets) and a 12-in battery (two double-barrelled armoured turrets) at close quarters from each other; b) at Suurupi one 14-in battery with two double-barrelled armoured turrets; c) at Aegna one 12-in battery with two double-barrelled armoured turrets. This heavy weaponry was destined for both sealing the entrance to the Gulf of Finland, as well as for the defence of the approaches to Paldiski. In the northerly and northeasterly directions 11-in mortars had been planned to be positioned on Naissaar island and Viimsi peninsula. Soon, however, the evaluation of the situation changed, demanding fundamental corrections to the plans. The new location and armament plan of the batteries was much more suited to the purpose than the initial one.

Naissaar Position

The main body of the workers were brought to the island in 1913. The accommodation was in shacks. When Naissaar islanders left their island in June 1914, the workers were accommodated in their abandoned houses. The first job that was undertaken was the building of a narrow-gauge railway and a port. Quite a dense railway network was built on the island. It connected the central port on the east coast with both Põhjaküla (North Village) and Lõunaküla (South Village), but also the batteries on the west coast and in the centre of the island. It was 750 mm in gauge and the total length of the lines, including sidings, was 37.7 km in 1918. The main railway installations were situated in Põhjaküla in the northern part of the island. A junction resembling a station was built there, with a wooden boarded shed for the two locomotives, a fire station and repair shops. Near the junction there were two batteries and the central command post to which separate tracks led from the station. In 1914, when the pier of the central port had been completed, the first locomotive was brought on to the island. It had been built by the O&K company in the same year. It was a 90 HP 0-6-0 tank like the ones used at Tahkuna. For nearly a year it played a solo role in the building of the fortifications, then another tank locomotive was brought to the island. That loco, built by the Tampella flax and engineering factory in 1907, had formerly belonged to the Hyvinkää-Karkkala private railway where it had been designated as No 1. The 90 HP locomotive was a 0-6-2 and weighed 14.5 tonnes, which permitted it to be used on the island's light type of railway. The 5-tonne two-axle flat wagons were brought up from Pärnu after the Waldof factory was liquidated; in addition there were some 8-tonne four-axle flat wagons made by Artur Koppel of St. Petersburg and some 10-tonne four-axle covered vans made at various Russian factories. By 1917 six batteries had been completed on Naissaar, one had been put into storage and two were under construction.

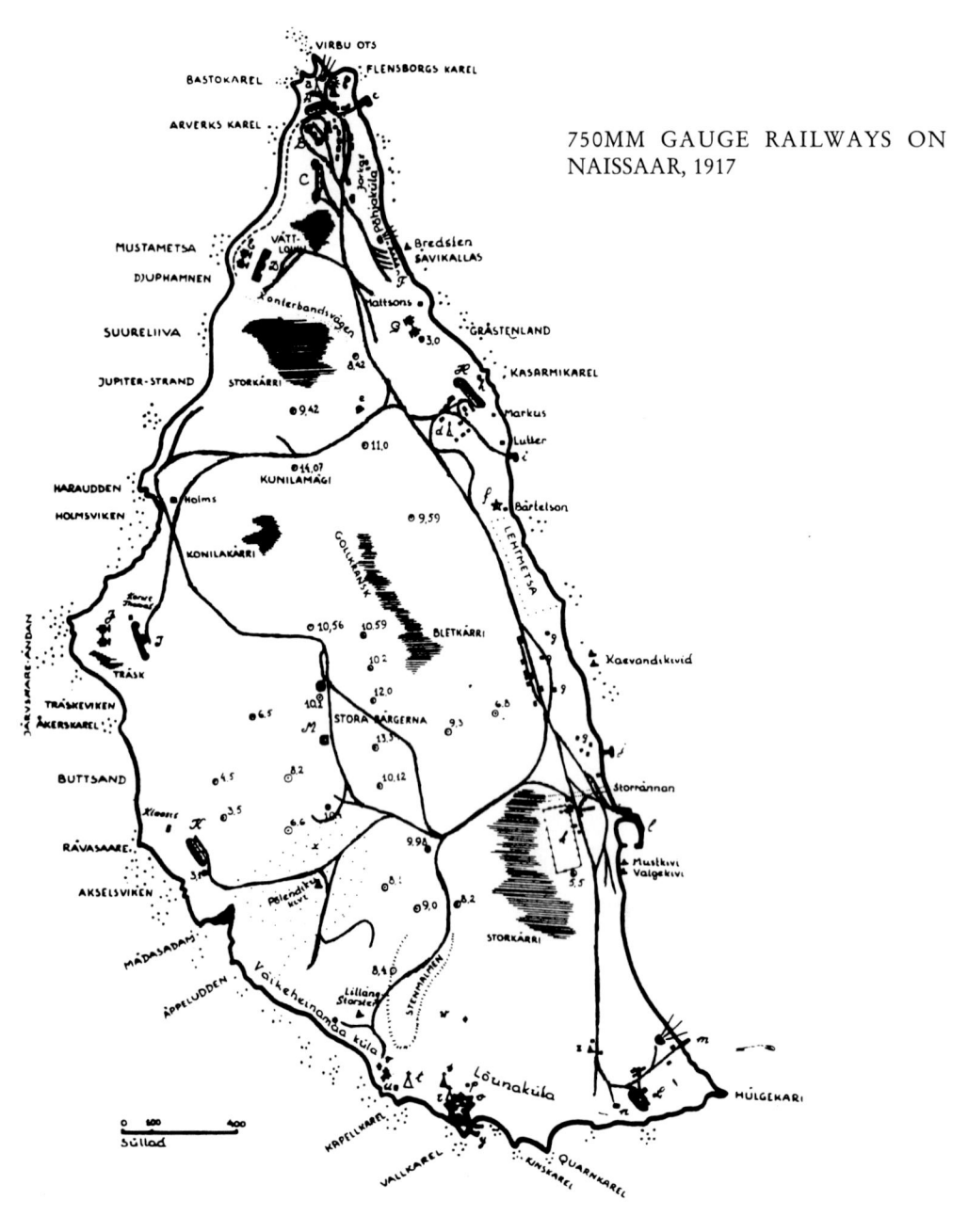

750MM GAUGE RAILWAYS ON NAISSAAR, 1917

Suurupi position

The military assignments of the Suurupi and Naissaar positions were nearly the same, and to a large extent the two positions supported each other. As on Naissaar the decision was made to build a temporary battery before permanent ones were constructed. The temporary battery was erected about 50 m from the shore, near Ilmandu village on the northwestern coast of the peninsula. When the Suurupi batteries Nos 2 and 3 were completed the temporary battery was dismantled. According to plans a 14-in armoured turret battery was to be built 300 metres to the south of the upper lighthouse. Only the gun emplacement pit could be dug there, however. As the work did not progress, it was decided to stop it altogether in spring 1916. Also at batteries Nos 2 and 3 some work was left unfinished. Two double-barrelled armoured turrets were set up on the Sôrve peninsula. The railway to Suurupi branched off the main line at Sôrve station on the Tallinn-Vääna line. The tracks headed northwest from Sôrve, passed Rannamôisa church and descended slowly down the cliff. Suurupi station was built at the foot of the cliff near the lighthouse (the building still stands there). From there side tracks led to each of the two batteries. The rolling stock, the engines and the wagons, were from the main line of the fortress railway. There was no separate rolling stock at Suurupi.

Aegna Position

Aegna was of secondary importance in the defence system of the Tallinn-Porkkala line, though far from being unimportant. Its firing sector covered Muuga Bay, the sea routes of the Gulf of Finland, as well as Tallinn Bay. Also at Aegna building was begun in the late autumn of 1914. The erection of the main batteries, however, did not start before 1915 and the weapons were finally installed only in 1917. Two 12-in double-barrelled armoured turrets had been planned to be installed in battery No 15. The erection of battery No 14 at the eastern coast progressed quickly. The concrete structures were completed later in the same year, only the arrival of the necessary armaments took longer. In 1913 the building of a narrow-gauge railway was started on the island, to connect the port on the southern coast with the batteries on the west and the north coasts, through the very centre of the island. The total length

5. Aegna's first locomotive, O&K 45HP 0-4-0WT locomotive No T118 of 1913.

of the railway was nearly 3 km. A shed for two locomotives was built in the centre of the island where also the barracks were located. About half the railway planned to be built on the island was completed in 1913, and the rest in the following year. The first locomotive on Aegna island was a 45 HP 0-4-0 tank, built in 1913 by O&K of Germany. The next year another locomotive, a 90 HP 0-6-0 tank, was added - the same type as the ones used on Naissaar and at Tahkuna. The flat wagons were the same kind used on Naissaar island; a few 10-tonne covered vans were also in use.

Paljassaar Position

Together with the Miidurand battery, battery No 12 with its 120 mm guns at the northwestern end of Suur-Paljassaar island made up the the last defence line of the naval fortress. It formed an essential part of the long east-west line of firing positions and concrete shelters.*

There was a railway siding to each gun emplacement and concrete shelter, connecting them to the main line. The main line first headed west from the gun emplacements, then continued south along the west coast and finally turned east, making a big circle. There was a pier on the east coast of Paljassaar on which the railway ended. The total length of the Paljassaare railway was 850 fathoms (2.81 km) and it was built in 1913. There were two engines in use on the line. They were brought there from the main lines. Most probably the engines used were 0-4-0 type 45 HP tank engines built by O&K in 1912-1913. These engines had been brought from St. Petersburg to give a hand in the building of the Tallinn Naval Fortress. The wagons were the same kind as used on Naissaar and Aegna Islands.

Supply System of the Sea Front

Like every fortification the sea front required ammunition for its batteries. The limestone cliffs area from Kadaka village to Tabasalu was chosen as the location of the depots. They were to be U-shaped and cut into stone at approximately 10 m depth. Each pair of tunnels, with the openings 50 m apart, was to be joined at the back, and the tunnels were to be wide enough to accommodate two trolley tracks running side by side. However, the changing situation also influenced the plans for the building of the tunnels. The initial plan was to build 33 to 39 tunnels (36 were finally settled on), with intervals of 100 to 150 metres between them. Slicing of the funds brought the number down to 15. Work started in 1916 by clearing the land under the cliff. On 10 November the initial plan was cut back once again, which meant that only 6 U-shaped tunnels would be dug in the cliff from the so-called Kadaka rise to near Paldiski Road. At first the work proceeded quite nicely. Tunnel No 3 was completed and two more tunnels were half completed. Also a ditch for a railway was dug at the foot of the cliff. Then it was decided that tunnels Nos 5 and 6 would be abandoned as their digging had only just begun and time was running short and there were other tunnels to be completed. On 27 June all work on the site came to a halt because financing of the project stopped. This started an argument about the future of the depots. Meanwhile one of the tunnels had been more or less completed and was handed over to the Russian Navy who demanded access to two more tunnels on 28 June. Their claim was partly successful. A railway was built to connect the depots with the naval fortress. It branched off the line leading to Kopli, near the crossing of Rahumäe tee and Tuisu Street, heading west in a big arch and passing the cannon depot (at present beside the first-aid hospital in Sütiste Street) in the general direction of Mustamägi. From there the railway passed across Habersti Road (now Ehitajate tee) and ran a couple of hundred metres parallel to it till its slantwise crossing of the present Üliôpilaste tee. Farther on, the railway passed between the present Tallinn Technical University and its stadium, heading directly towards the foot of the cliff just before the openings of the depots. After running past the openings the railway ascended to the top of the cliff and then joined the main railway line at a place about a kilometre from the Nômme-Väike station. As there was a war going on and the Germans were approaching Tallinn, the depots had to be disposed of so they wouldn't fall prey to the enemy. The tunnel openings were blown up, covering them with earth. The railway remained, though it was no longer used. In 1920 the line was taken up from the Rahumäe tee crossing to the openings of the tunnels.

* The two Paljassaar islands were turned into a peninsula in the course of the building, the channel between the island and the mainland being filled up.

Chapter 5
The Tallinn Naval Fortress - Land Defences

The naval fortress also had to be defended on the land side. For that purpose a number of defence installations were erected also inland around Tallinn. Most of them were linked to the fortress railway main lines which made up a dense network around Tallinn.

Defence Centre, No 1
The building of this defence installation started 250 m to the south of the Vääna-Viti manor centre. The biggest command post of the land front was set up there, complete with concrete shelters and firing positions. A narrow-gauge railway was brought up to the defence centre from the Sôrve-Suurupi line as a continuation of the railway to the Suurupi batteries which were never built. In 1920 the branch line was taken up.

Defence Position No 2
There were plans to build this position at Liikva, on the edge of the low Vääna cliff, but as time ran short work at the position was never completed. A part of the project that was completed was a branch railway line. It started at Vääna station, and was taken up in 1920.

Defence Position No 3
The position was located in the sandy area between Liikva, Vatsla and Sôrve. In the time and space available some concrete installations were built there and one 12-in cannon was set up in a round emplacement. A narrow-gauge railway was built to the position from Vatsla station on the Tallinn-Vääna main line. The length of the branch line was about 2 km. Here also the line was taken up by 1922, after the firing position had been dismantled.

Defence Position No 4
Initially the position was to be located at Kodasema Village, but the plan proved unsound from the tactical point of view. The Fortress Building Department decided that Kodasema could have no importance in terms of defence. So the idea of any further fortification of the area was abandoned and the position was transferred to Peetrimôisa Heights. A stretch of railway had been built, however, branching off the Vääna main line between Vatsla and Sôrve stations. Also a cobblestone road was built from Harku (parts of it have been preserved). The Vääna-Peetri position was located to both sides of the Tallinn-Paldiski road, at Vääna-Posti. It was another position that could not be completed because time was running short. Only the reinforced concrete command post and concrete shelters were built. The digging of the firing position foundations was started, but never completed. A narrow-gauge railway was built to the position from Harku station on the Vääna main line. From the station the branch line headed in the direction of Alliku village where it made an arch to the west and north to Peetri. From Peetri there were sidings to the Vääna-Posti positions, forming a loop. That railway line was used by the military as late as the 1930s.

Defence Position No 5
According to plans which largely remained on paper the position was to be built on Vene-Kabelimägi Hill between Harku and Hüüru. Only a 12-in howitzer battery was installed near Hüüru Manor, and a narrow-gauge railway was taken there from Harku station. It was a short branch line which branched off the Harku-Alliku-Peetri line. The line existed as late as the 1930s.

Defence Position No 6
The position was centred on the Pääsküla alvar. Six large concrete shelters were built there. In the rear of the position a 12-in gun emplacement was built (still to be seen at the end of the present Olevi Street) between the crests of the sand dunes there. To facilitate ammunition transport to the gun a trolley track was taken to the emplacement from a railway branch line. The latter branched off the Tallinn-Pärnu private railway at Valdeku station, running from there along the edge of Pääsküla bog to the position. The railway line was taken up by 1922.

Defence Position No 7

The position was built in the area between Pääsküla and the Männiku bog, about 150 meters in the direction of the city from Männiku station. Emplacements for two 12 in-cannon were built a couple of hundred metres north of the station. A railway branch line was built there from the station, and was later extended to the future magazine. The line remained in service for a long time (see below).

Defence Position No 8

The position embraced the area between the villages of Raudalu and Saidre and was divided into two sectors: fortified post E between the Tallinn-Viljandi road and Männiku bog, and fortified post Zh to the east of the Tallinn-Viljandi road. Each post had four cannon in flat depressions surrounded by sand banks. Also a command post and shelters were built for the position. The position was linked to the railway by a branch line from Liiva station on the Tallinn-Pärnu private railway. Three sidings were laid down, and a new limestone station building and water tower were built in the typical fortress design, instead of the wooden shack which formerly served as the station building. So the former Liiva halt became Liiva station. The siding branched off the easternmost track of Liiva station, running parallel to the Tallinn-Viljandi road until it forked into two at Raudalu village. The siding was in existence as late as the early 1930s.

Defence Position No 12

The territory of the position was supposed to stretch from Nehatu-Loo near Tallinn to Muuga Bay. Most of the project remained uncompleted - only the trenches were dug, along with 3 kilometres of communication tunnels. Also some batteries were installed. The heavy howitzer battery beside the Kose Hospital School on the bank of the Pirita River opposite the Iru fort hill should be mentioned here. Also various ferro-concrete structures and depots were built there. The railway link to the position started at the Iru barracks. As regards the railway to Iru, it branched off at the present Ülemiste station (formerly Lasna station) on the Tallinn-St. Petersburg railway. The line ran diagonally across what is now the Pae Street quarter of the Lasnamäe residential district, then ran across land that was later taken into use as an

6. An incomplete gun installation at Nõmme. Ammunition was hoisted to the gun's magazine by crane. The crane beams are visible in the picture.

airfield and from there to the high riverbank at Iru. The railway to the defence position crossed the river by a bridge beside what is now a home for the aged (the bridge pillars still stand today). A light battery for the protection of the bridge was located in a primitive emplacement on the left bank of the river. The rail line was very short-lived, for the temporary firing positions were dismantled soon.

Defence Positions That Were Never Built

Positions No 9 at Lehmja Village, No 10 at Rae and No 11 near Lagedi Manor remained only on paper. Only a narrow-gauge railway was laid down to the village of Lehmja where there was a fork. After completion the railway was to connect the Rae and the Lagedi positions. The siding started at the Tallinn-Väike station where a typical limestone station was built. From there it headed in the direction of Ülemiste along what is now Veduri Street and parts of Kaare tee, running parallel to the standard-gauge Tallinn-Tapa railway, and arching round Lake Ülemiste after which it ran along the present Tallinn-Tartu highway to Lehmja Village. There are reports of a partial survival of the line up to the 1930s. Also the firing positions and depots started in Tallinn (at Nômme and Mustamäe) remained uncompleted. These were mostly intended for naval defence however. There are two such positions known in Nômme - one on the sand dunes opposite Nômme market, and the other at the end of Suurtüki Street at Hiiu. The main line of the Tallinn-Vääna railway ran past the position located opposite the Nômme market, the connection with it being directly by a short track branching off the main line. Obviously there were intentions to build an anti-aircraft battery or an ammunition depot in the square near the firing position. Also that location was connected with the main railway line by a siding branching off the Rahumäe triangle. A branch line also led to the Hiiu position. It branched off the Vääna main line approximately at the site of the present Mustamäe ski jump. The Mustamäe depots were made up of two caponiers located side by side, with a distance of a couple of hundred metres between them, along what is now Sütiste tee. The depots were surrounded by high sand banks. A railway network was built there, and the connection was by a line which branched off the side track from Tondi to the Kadaka ammunition tunnels. There were military barracks near the depots, and later, a polygon (at present a sports ground).

Giant Magazine at Männiku

The Tallinn Naval Fortress land front system also required magazines to store ammunition. The idea to build a giant magazine was born in the Fortress Building Department. The magazine was built on the high sand bank of the Pääsküla bog, parallel with the narrow-gauge Tallinn-Pärnu private railway. Later an ammunition factory was set up there. The railway connection to it was by an extension of the

7. The spur leading to the giant Männiku magazine.

THE RAIL NETWORK OF THE MÄNNIKU MAGAZINE

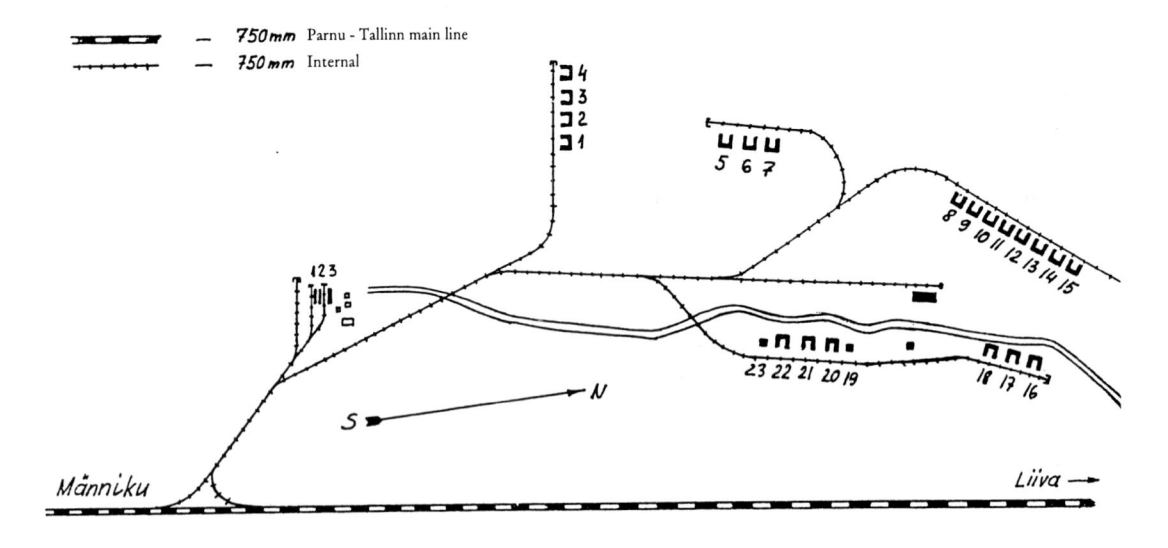

railway to position No 7. It was a ramified network of lines, of which one extended to Männiku station and the other to Valdeku halt. Later the track to Valdeku was taken up. The network towards Männiku station was in service up to the middle 1970s.

New Land Front Positions and their Railway Connections

It was found in 1915 that the defence installations erected for the land front were much too near Tallinn as well as points of major strategic importance, particularly the giant magazine at Männiku. Immediately orders came from St. Petersburg to start shifting the advance positions forward by 2 to 4 versts, without delay. The fortress builders now decided to further fortify positions Nos 1, 2 and 3 by adding new installations, and to build entirely new positions between Türisalu and Tôlinômme and at Humala, as well as one more fortified post at Vahiküla. Plans were made for creating defence installations in the Rae and Loo area, around Lagedi, Jüri and Lehmja, etc. Entirely new positions were created on the Viimsi Peninsula and in the Lasnamäe area (near the Hundikuristik gully). Proportionally, the fortress railways network was expanded. All this happened at a tremendous rate.

Humala Defence Position

The drawings for the position were completed by the summer of 1916. Three big shelters were built in the time available, and work was started on a fourth one. There were several batteries at the position, of which one was located a considerable distance away - on high ground beside the road leading from Vääna to Vääna-Posti. The concrete installations are still there today, but the ground around them has been trucked away to be used as road filler. A railway line was built to the position from Vääna station. At Humala it forked into several directions, each branch to one of the defence installations. The line existed until the middle 1930s.

Türisalu - Naage Position

The position was never fully built. Only one shelter could be put up near the village of Naage. In neighbouring Vaila depressions for the gun emplacements were sunk, concrete shelters for the crew were built and communication tunnels (trenches) between the positions and the command post were dug. In addition, ditches for the railway link were cut in the limestone cliff near Vääna station and at Türisalu. A stretch of railway was laid down from Vääna station to Vaila and on the rise onto the cliff beside the village. The railway was dismantled in 1920.

Alliku Defence Position

This was created for the fortification of Position No 4. The new position was situated a short distance to the south of Alliku village. A straight cobbled road was built there from Paldiski. As the Alliku position was never completed, only one of the shelters was built. A railway had already been taken to Alliku in connection with the building of position No 4. As it now had two positions to serve, it was decided to erect a station at Alliku. A stone station building in the typical fortress design was put up, which is still there today. The branch line existed as late as the 1930s.

Tammemäe Defence Position

The position established near Juuliku between Saue and Saku was a forward defence post of defensive position No 6. Only trenches could be dug there before work was called off. Still, a railway was laid down to the position in the time and space available. It branched off the section between Männiku and Saku stations on the Tallinn-Pärnu private railway, and was dismantled in 1920.

Saku Defence Position

The position was born by moving position No 7 forward from the ammunition magazine. Trenches were dug there, stretching as far as Saku brewery workers' tenements. Also five 240-mm Japanese mortars were installed at the position. A railway to the position was built directly from Saku station. The line was taken up in 1920.

Nômme Village Defence Position

The position was created by shifting the front line south of the Saidre-Raudalu area. The position was located on either side of the Tallinn-Viljandi road, near the crossing leading to Saku. A narrow-gauge railway was built there - an extension of the Liiva-Raudalu branch. The line forked at Razdelnaya stop, one of the branches crossing the road to Viljandi, passing close to Nômme village and then heading towards Kurna. The other line ran parallel with the road to Viljandi, passed Tammesalu and then forked once again: one of the two branches went direct to Sausti and the other to a point west of that village. A fortress railway station, Nômme-Lôuna, was laid out there. It consisted of three tracks and a wooden station building. A reinforced concrete emplacement for three 240 mm Japanese mortars was built near the railway station. The railway was dismantled in the 1920s.

8. Russian sailors and artillerymen.

(Plateway Press)

9. A general view of Nômme-Väike station, the hub of the 75cm gauge network. Note 5ft gauge tracks in foreground and the wooden station building.

10. Männiku station, a typical structure built from local limestone.

Chapter 6
Railways of the Tallinn Naval Fortress

The railway serving the sea and land front fortifications was built to 750 mm gauge. It consisted of two totally independent networks in Tallinn and its vicinity, together with lines branching off the Tallinn-Pärnu private railway. The building of the fortress railway started in 1913. It was extremely labour-intensive work. Embankments and depressions, bridges and flyovers (to cross the broad-gauge railway at Rahumäe in Tallinn) were needed, as well as an engine shed corresponding to the needs of the fortress, water towers, stations and various other auxiliary buildings. Most of the labour was brought from Russia, and the men's living conditions were far below standard. Local workers were also employed. Traffic on the Nômme-Fortress-Sôrve-Suurupi line was opened in the summer of 1913, the section from Nômme to Sôrve being double track. Further lines built in 1913-1917: Nômme-Fortress-Liiva, Sôrve-Vääna-Humala, Harku-Alliku-Peetri-Alliku, Rahumäe-Kopli, Liiva-Raudalu-Kurna/Sausti, Tondi-Mustamäe-Kadaka, Tallinn-Väike-Ülemiste-Lehmja, Lasna-Iru-Kose, Valdeku-Pääsküla-Laagri, Kôrgemäe-Kodasema, Rannamôisa-Vääna-Viti, Vääna-Türisalu (not completed by 1917), Paljassaar island, Aegna island, Naissaar island. By the end of 1914 the total length of the railways extended to 103, by the end of 1915 to 178 and of 1916 to 228.5 km. In 1919 there were 106 km of main lines, and 263 km of track (incl. sidings). The plans envisaged the building of 250 km of railways on the mainland, but the target was never met. The figure given as the total length of the railways by German occupation authorities was 244.7 km, which is additional proof of the fact that not all lines indicated on the map were actually built. The lengths of the separate lines were as follows:

Nômme - Harku	5.34 km	Baltika - Kopli	2.67 km
Harku - Sôrve	7.81 km	Tondi - Kadaka (Mäeküla)	7.36 km
Sôrve - Vatsla	2.13 km	Kadaka - Harku	4.42 km
Vatsla - Vääna	2.74 km	Valdeku - Pääsküla	9.92 km
Vatsla - Liikva	2.58 km	Liiva - Razdelnaya	5.67 km
Vääna - Humala	3.71 km	Razdelnaya - Tammetalu	1.39 km
Vääna - Türisalu	4.91 km	Tammetalu - Sausti	4.47 km
Sôrve - Suurupi	4.59 km	Sausti - Nômme-Lôuna	2.67 km
Suurupi - lighthouse	2.45 km	Razdelnaya - Saidre	1.07 km
Suurupi - Viti	2.46 km	Saidre - Kurna	2.35 km
Harku - Alliku	5.01 km	Tallinn-Väike - Rae	9.5 km
Alliku - Peetri	3.73 km	Rae - Loo	1.77 km
Alliku - Lehmja	1.49 km	Dvigatel - Iru	8.32 km
Nômme - Nômme-Ida	2.14 km	Liiva - Tallinn-Väike	2.18 km
Nômme-Ida - Liiva	2.19 km	Tallinn-Väike - Tallinn Port	3.73 km
Nômme-Ida - Tondi	2.67 km	Picket No 65 - Kose	1.71 km
Tondi - Baltika	3.09 km	Picket No 33 - Kadrintal	1.17 km

Of the sea front positions only Suurupi had a direct link with the mainland. The railways on Naissaar, Aegna and Paljassaar islands were autonomous. Their building started in 1913. There were no stations on the island railways, except a junction with primitive wooden motive power sheds in the northern part of Naissaar.

Stations

There were 38 stations altogether, including halts. The principal type of station was built of local limestone, usually with wooden auxiliary buildings. The first stations were built to a standard design. They were outwardly similar to each other, with only some minor differences. At Liiva and Sôrve there

THE TALLINN NAVAL
FORTRESS   RAILWAY
NETWORK

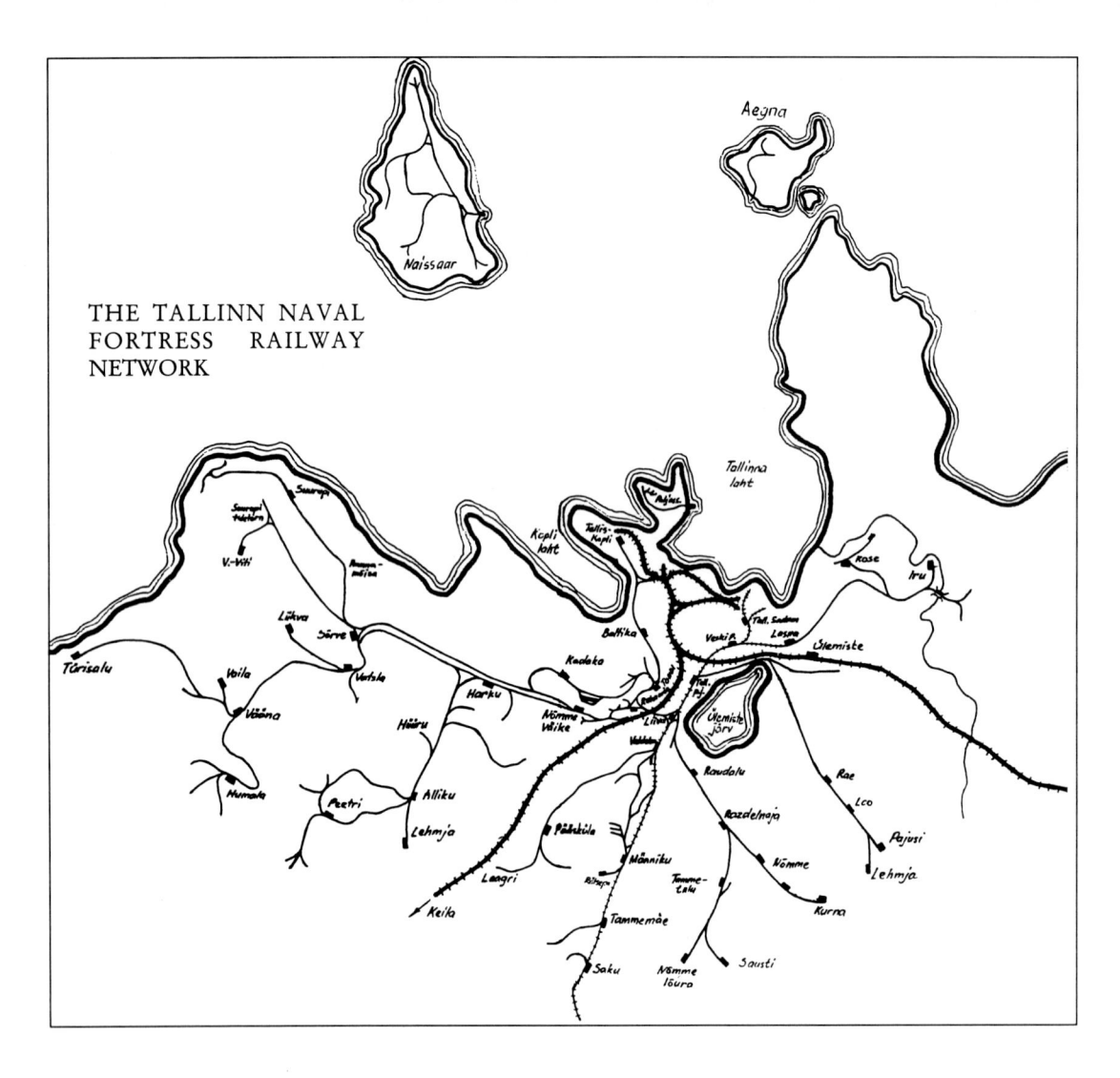

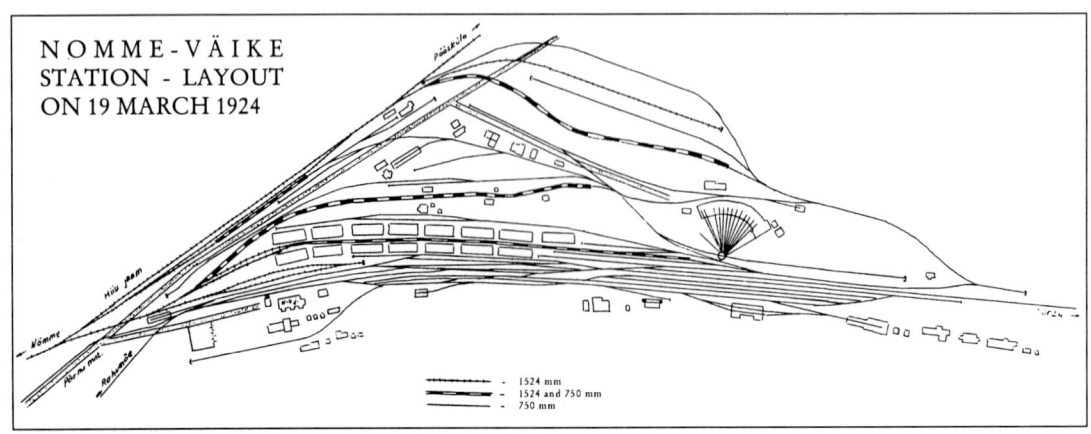

NOMME-VÄIKE
STATION - LAYOUT
ON 19 MARCH 1924

- 1524 mm
- 1524 and 750 mm
- 750 mm

were also limestone water towers. The other buildings were built of wood, and only their foundations have survived. The main station on the fortress railway was Nômme-Kindluse (Nômme-Ida, later Nômme II and Nômme-Väike), which was located at Hiiu. As an exception the station building was built of wood. There were large warehouses and a locomotive shed in the area of the station. Several broad-gauge tracks coming from the main Nômme station intertwined with the multitude of narrow-gauge lines. These started at the main Nômme station. A narrow-gauge line went from Nômme-Kindluse station also to the main Nômme station. The station buildings have survived till today. The station at Vääna (built of wood) is used today as the local post office, although originally it was used as a barracks. The house was taken into use as a station only between the two world wars.

Roundhouse

A modern roundhouse accommodating seventy locomotives was built beside the main station of the fortress. It had a circular ground plan with 25 stalls and a swivel bridge. Work on it was finished only in the summer of 1919, an event which also marked the completion of the Tallinn Naval Fortress railway system, even though by that time most of the lines had lost their importance. In 1922 part of the roundhouse (5 stalls) was dismantled. By 1924 15 stalls were left. This is how the building has been preserved. The contraction of the roundhouse was because of a fall in the number of locomotives on the fortress railway.

11. Water crane at Sôrve, with the water tower in the background.

12. A general view of the twenty-stall roundhouse at Nômme, 1922.

13. A close up view of part of Nômme roundhouse, 1922.

14. Nõmme roundhouse after five stalls had been demolished in 1924.

15. Nõmme locomotive depot drivers, 1920.

16. O&K 90HP 0-6-0 No T108 of 1914, with the tender of locomotive W3 attached.

17. O&K 50HP 0-6-0WT locomotive of 1914.

Chapter 7
Locomotives and Rolling Stock

The fortress railway rolling stock was varied. In 1913 the Arthur Koppel works at St. Petersburg built some 8-tonne four-axle flat wagons, 12-tonne covered vans as well as mail vans and coaches for the fortress railway. In 1915 when the Waldhof factory was liquidated over one hundred 5-tonne two-axle flat wagons were handed over to the fortress railway. In 1920 the fortress railway had a total of 38 coaches and 1,392 freight wagons. The locomotives came from an even more varied stock. By early 1918 there were 73 locomotives in all. The first of them were 0-4-0WTs built in 1912-1913 by O&K. A good number of those locomotives had been ordered for the Emperor Peter the Great Naval Fortress through the agency of the Arthur Koppel works at St. Petersburg. Six were dispatched from here for the construction of the naval fortress in Tallinn. Additionally, two such locomotives were ordered specially for the fortress in Tallinn in 1913. One, O&K 6780/13 was sent to Aegna Island, while the other, No 7503/14, was assigned to the giant magazine at Männiku. Two of the first six locomotives worked at Paljassaar. In 1914 nine 90 HP and eight 50 HP 0-6-0 type tank locomotives arrived from the same company. Of the more powerful locomotives one was dispatched to Naissaar and another to Aegna Island. One went to the Môntu-Sôrve line on Saaremaa and two to the Tahkuna-Lehtma line on Hiiumaa. Of the less powerful locomotives two were sent to the Kuivastu-Vôi line on Muhu island and one to Vormsi island.

The same year five O&K Company heavy 0-10-0s (Nos 7205-7209) arrived for the fortress railway in Tallinn. Rated at 325 HP they were intended for the transportation of heavy naval cannon from one position to another. Because of its heavy weight and great power such a locomotive could haul quite a long train. In 1915 four 0-8-0 tank locomotives passed into the command of the fortress railway. Having previously served at the Waldhof factory in Pärnu before it was liquidated, these 100 HP locomotives had been built by Krauss & Co. in 1899-1909 (Nos 4034/99, 4696/02, 5175/05 and 6099/09). The same year two locomotives were also bought from Finland, one from the Forssa-Humpilla and the other from the Hyvinkää—Karkkila line. The former, a 2-8-2 type 100 HP tank locomotive, was built in 1900 by the Baldwin Locomotive Works, USA. As an exception to the other tank locomotives its traction wheels were located inside the frame. The local engineers nicknamed it *"ämblik"* (the spider), obviously because of its appearance. The Hyvinkää-Karkkila locomotive, No 1, had been built in 1907 at the Tampere (Tammersfors) Flax and Engineering Factory (Tampella No 124). This 0-6-2 tank locomotive was transferred to Naissaar Island in 1915 where it worked up to 1944.

As World War I broke out, it was no longer possible for Russia to order new locomotives from Germany, because the countries were now at war with each other. At the same time there was a pressing need for more locomotives on the fortress railway system. Then the imperial government came to an agreement with the Americans who agreed to sell armaments, and other supplies including locomotives, to Russia. The first consignment of narrow-gauge locomotives for the Tallinn Naval Fortress was ordered at the beginning of 1915 from Alco. The same year a consignment of lightweight 2-6-0 tender locomotives (Nos 55400-55411) were built. Twelve of the locomotives, designated 1-12, were shipped to Tallinn. En route to Tallinn, however, the ship carrying the first six locomotives sank, hit by a German torpedo. To replace the ones lost six modernised locomotives (Nos 56766-56771) were dispatched to Tallinn under the old numbers. That way the locomotives built in 1916 were designated Nos 1-6 and those built in 1915 Nos 7-12. These locomotives were rated at 90 HP. In 1917 the same company built eight 0-6-0 universal tank locomotives for the Peter the Great Naval Fortress. Of these, three locomotives arrived in Estonia where they were designated by the series W (B) Nos. 1-3. Later sixty such locomotives (Nos 71-130) were built for Russian field railways. Twenty-one of them (1-8 and 71-83) were shipped to Russia, but with the onset of the Bolshevik revolution, no more were delivered. Subsequently the remaining locomotives were sold off to customers all over the world. Unfortunately the engines were of a poor design and had to be repaired quite often. However, their detachable tenders were successfully used with the Koppel tank locomotives for decades afterwards.

18. Baldwin 2-8-2T No T101 was purchased from the Jokionen-Forssa railway of Finland.

19. A 100HP 0-8-0T built by Krauss & Co. in 1905, obtained from the demolished Waldhof woodpulp factory in Pärnu.

20. A 90HP A class 2-6-0 built by Alco in 1915.

21. A 90HP A class 2-6-0 built by Alco in 1916.

22. Alco W(B) class 0-6-0WT locomotive built in 1917.

In 1916 the Kolomna engineering works in Russia commenced production of 60 HP 0-6-0 universal field railway locomotives. The factory defined the locomotives as type 86, but on field railways they were classed as belonging to the N (H) series. The first consignment of such locomotives had already been built in 1904. Six N series locomotives were also shipped to Tallinn for use on the naval fortress railway. According to reports by the local people the locomotives were painted brown and nicely "made up". The locomotives were designated universal because they could be used both with tender and as tank locomotives. In 1917 a 40 HP 0-6-0WT was brought over from the Rakke limeworks. It had been built by Borsig in Germany in 1914 (No 8976), originally for 762 mm gauge. When it was transferred to the fortress railway the gauge had to be changed. There are reports of several other types of locomotives dispatched for the Tallinn Naval Fortress, but because of the lack of archival records it has not been possible to establish any firm details about their activity there. For example seventy 0-6-0 tanks numbered 1-70 (56324-56363) were ordered by the Russian Ministry of War from Alco. Initially they were destined for the Russian field railway in Poland. However, as the German army had swiftly advanced from Poland into Russian territory the locomotives were sent to the port of Narvik in Norway, and from there to Tornio in Finland. There the locomotives were loaded on Russian railway wagons, destination Tallinn. It is not known, however, whether any of them ever arrived there. In fact, some of the locomotives turned up on the Sarikam-Erzurum railway in Turkey in 1920. That railway had already been built by the Russians during the Russo-Turkish war. There are records showing that in 1914 four 0-8-0 tank locomotives were built by the O&K factory which were at first dispatched to the Kaunas fortress, but as the Kaunas railway was built to 600 mm gauge the locos were diverted to Tallinn. Whether they ever reached Tallinn and what became of them is not known.

Retreating before the German advance, the Russian army was compelled to continuously evacuate its property, including that of the field railway. In one such evacuation operation fourteen French-built 0-6-0 type Russian field railway locomotives of the M series arrived at the Tallinn Naval Fortress in 1916. They were 70 HP lightweight locomotives with tender ordered during the Russo-Japanese war and built at several French factories in 1905-1906. Five of them were assigned to the building of the Paide-Tamsalu field railway by the Russian military authorities. In 1918 the Germans brought two more such locomotives from Poland, and they too were put to service at the building of the Paide-Tamsalu field railway which the Russians had not managed to complete. All together, 16 such locomotives were registered in the books of the Nômme locomotive depot.

23. A 60HP N(86) class 0-6-0T built in Kolomna, Russia, and equipped with auxiliary tender.

24. 0-6-0WT No T112 (Rt237) built by Borsig in 1914 and obtained from the lime works at Rakke.

25. 70HP 0-6-0 No M113 built by Batignolles for the Russian Ministry of War in 1906.

26. A 12-in gun battery after the German assault in the autumn of 1917.

27. A destroyed 12-in gun at Naissaar in 1918.

28. Construction work in progress on the 60cm gauge 'Feldbahn' railway at Lladjala, Saaremaa in 1918.

Chapter 8
The Railways under German Occupation (1918-1919)

The German occupation of 1917-1918 began with the invasion of the West-Estonian islands. The demoralised Russian coast defence units were unable to offer sufficient resistance. Some of the batteries on the islands didn't manage to fire a single shot. Only the Sôrve and Vôi batteries offered weak resistance. Having fired a few shots the batteries were blown up and the crews retreated to the mainland. Because of the hurried retreat some batteries fell into German hands undamaged. The Tahkuna and Lehtma batteries on Hiiumaa island had a similar fate. Batteries Nos 39 (Tahkuna) and 38 (Lehtma) were partly demolished. Battery No 37 at Lehtma was abandoned without serious damage in February 1918. Also the batteries on Vormsi island were blasted and the crews took to flight. As if by a miracle the railways at Sôrve-Sääre, Muhu, Tahkuna and Vormsi survived the takeover. All the locomotives were left in working order and were taken over by the Germans. On 16/17 February 1918 the military began packing up also at the Tallinn Naval Fortress positions. Blasting teams were sent to the coastguard batteries where the demolition operation took place on 24 and 26 February. Nervous haste did not permit the operation to be carried out with good results. On Naissaar island the blasting team wanted to be smart and connected the charges to the exisiting telephone network, with the switch at the central port. But the local forester outsmarted them, cutting as many of the wires as he could. So only batteries Nos 5, 7, 9, 10b and 11 were damaged, some more, some less seriously. At Suurupi the buildings were burnt and battery No 2 was blasted. Also the installations at Kakumäe and battery No 15 on Aegna was blown up. The land front suffered very little. Just a few installations were blown up. Only the tunnel depot in the limestone cliffs at Kadaka village was seriously damaged. After its destruction the fortress practically ceased to exist. Fortunately all the railways and their rolling stock escaped destruction. They were taken over and put to use by the Germans.

The Germans take over.

By February 1918 the German imperial army had occupied the whole of Estonia's territory. The naval fortress installations and their railways passed into the new owners' command. In addition, the local German army command stationed a permanent garrison on both Naissaar and Aegna Islands, 50 men on either island. Two temporary batteries were formed on Naissaar, using cannon which had escaped destruction. As the railway had remained intact the Germans began using it for their own purposes. Aegna was considered to be more important than Naissaar by the occupation authorities, because now the enemy could be expected from the east. Plans were made for the restoration of the 12-in armoured turret, but could not be carried out because of the lack of materials. Then it was decided to lay out a new position next to the old one. It was built of concrete, making use of cannon salvaged from the anti-aircraft battery which had survived destruction. The position was also connected up with the railway. No shots were fired in battle from any of the three batteries, which quite well characterises the military situation at the time. The rest of the Tallinn Naval Fortress railway was used by the Germans for general purposes and their own military transport. Some of the locomotives were transferred to the building of the Paide-Tamsalu railway which was opened to traffic in autumn 1918. But like the Russians, the Germans were unable to complete the building of the railway and traffic on the line was halted when the Germans left.

"Feldbahn" railways

The Germans wanted to turn Saaremaa island into an impenetrable sea fortress in its own right. Therefore, besides taking over the batteries which had escaped destruction, a decision was also made to restore those batteries which had been blown up. To improve the provision of supplies and other services in the fortress it was decided to create a 600 mm field railway ("feldbahn") network focussing on Kuressaare. The railway was to start at Roomassaare port, and head from there to Kuressaare main station. From there one branch was to go via Upa and Putla to Orissaare, another from Putla to Soela, a

"FELDBAHN" RAILWAYS ON THE ISLAND OF SAAREMAA, 1918-1919

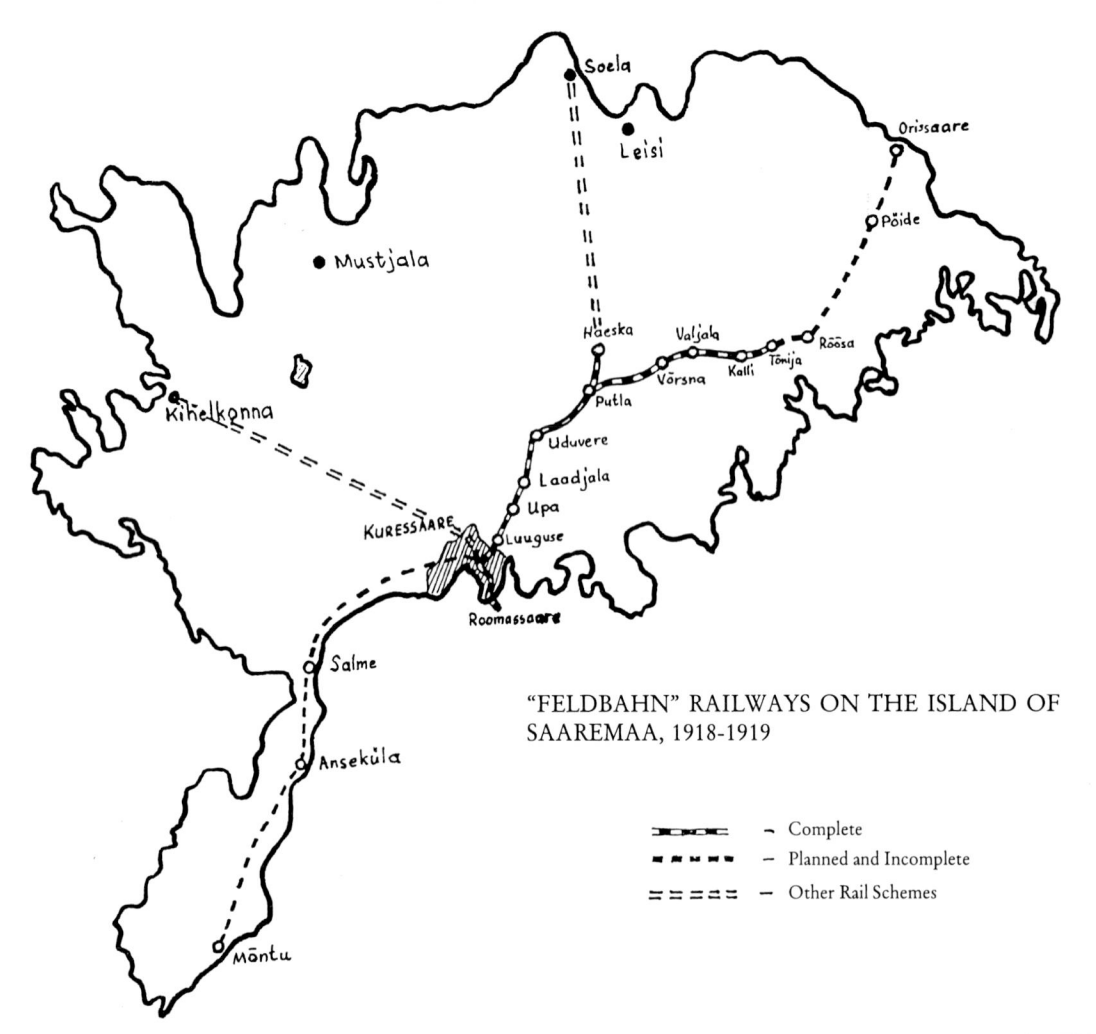

- Complete
- Planned and Incomplete
- Other Rail Schemes

29. Field railway locomotives on Sareemaa island. On the left is a 'feldbahn' 0-8-0T, while a 'Zwillinge' loco poses on the right.

third south from Kuressaare main station, and a fourth from Kuressaare to Môntu, to join the railway to Sôrve-Sääre. Building work was entrusted to a special railway building detachment. Mainly prisoners of war were used as labour in the construction, but also local inhabitants and even schoolchildren were employed.

The first stretch of the railway, between Kuressaare and Roomassaare port, was completed at the end of October 1917. Mainly stamped metal sleepers were used side by side with timber ones. The line started on the Roomassaare pier and forked into two after 3 km. One of the branches headed to the main station or the depot which was located in the area bordered by the present Pihtla tee, Talve and Jaama Streets. The other branch ran parallel to Vana-Roomassaare Street until Castle Park where it once more forked into two. The longer of the two branches ran along the coast, crossing Pargi Street to the ruins of Wildenberg's factory, while the shorter branch went from the Roomassaare mud bath unit straight into the park. In the park the tracks were laid directly on a footpath and the Kuursaal resort club was turned into a station. Next a 21.5 km stretch was built from Kuressaare to Putla and Haeska. It began at the main station. The stretch was completed in May 1918 and traffic was started immediately. There were six stations: Luuguse, Upa, Laadjala, Uduvere, Putla and Haeska. The tracks between Luuguse inn and the main station were placed directly on the highway, and further on on a special embankment. In June and July 1918 the course of the 40 km line from Putla to Orissaare via Valjala was marked out. Building started immediately afterwards. The embankment was built as far as Orissaare, with the exception of a few hundred metres between the manors of Pöide and Rôôsa. The track was laid over a 22 km stretch up to Rôôsa manor. Traffic started as soon as the stretch was completed.

Initially there were five stations: Putla, Vôrsna, Valjala, Kalli and Waldbahnhof (between Tônija and Rôôsa). Regular traffic was begun on the route from Kuressaare to Tônija in October 1919. The line had been built in a great hurry and so its condition was extremely poor, making a ride on the railway quite a dangerous affair. There were cases of engines or coaches leaving the track. But as the wagons were light, each locomotive was able to haul the wagons back on to the tracks after an accident. Maximum speed on the line was 15 kph. The line from Kuressaare to Anseküla and Môntu was marked out in June and July of the same year. Beginning at the main station, it ran through Salme, Anseküla and Tehumardi to Môntu where it was to join the railway built by the Russians which led from there to the Sôrve batteries. Of course the old rails had to be relaid to suit 600 mm gauge. However, the building of that stretch of railway was never completed, nor was the Sôrve battery ever restored. Railways had also been planned to batteries at Soela and Kihelkonna. The former route was to go via Haeska and the latter via Kuressaare main station. But here also the plans could not be carried out because of the Germans leaving the island. Starting from May 1918 private individuals were permitted to ride on the railway lines which had been put into operation. The price of a ride was established at 12 pfenning per kilometre in a second class coach and 8 pfenning third class.

Rolling Stock

The German occupation authorites brought 12 steam and 2 diesel locomotives for the stretches of railway built in 1917-1918. Most of the steam locos were 0-8-0 type, the so-called 'Feldbahn' engines built by Henschel & Sohn and O&K, but there were also other types (0-6-0 and 0-4-0) built by Krauss, Vulkan (Stettin) and Linke-Hoffmann. There were two small engines also from the Koppel factory. The field railway numbers of some of the locomotives established include: 0-8-0 'Feldbahn' engines - HF 1502 (Henschel No 15241/17), HF 1507 (Henschel No 15246/17), HF 1509 (Henschel No 15248/17), HF 1674 (O. & K. No 8374/17). Of the 0-6-0 type a Zwilling engine, HF 87, is known, built by Krauss & Co in 1895 (No 3157). The Vulkan engine belonged to the field railway series 894-900 built in 1916 (No 3214-3230/16). There were also two ambulance, 122 lumber and 125 flat wagons and 4 coaches with built-in stoves. In the 1920s the stock was complemented by two more coaches built at the local industrial school.

End of the German Occupation of Saaremaa

When the German monarchy fell the Germans started a hasty pullout of their troops from the occupied territories. This brought the building of railways on the island to a stop in November 1918 and its equipment was offered for sale. In December 1919 the occupants handed the railway over to the Kuressaare municipality over a contract whereby the town was given the priority right to use and purchase the rolling stock. A legal committee of the Ministry of Communications attested the contract as valid in 1921, but there were influencial people in the Ministry who preferred to ignore that opinion, saying the contract, drawn up in the German spirit, was fictitious. Some of the equipment was also taken back to Germany by the leaving troops.

The Germans depart

Like any occupation army, the Germans shipped away what they could at their departure. The engines from Môntu and Kuivastu (three altogether) were loaded on ships and taken to Germany. Fortunately the three locomotives at Tahkuna and Vormsi were not removed. The occupants also left Tallinn with some material belongings. So from the Nômme locomotive shed they took away rails to build 36 versts of track, complete with the fastenings, machines, tools and various other things from copper station bells to the fortress railways archives. Also a 0-6-0 tank No 4034/89 built in 1899 at the Krauss factory was taken along, and later turned up at the Zbiersk sugar factory in Poland. Another locomotive, a Koppel-built 50 HP 0-6-0, was taken to an unknown destination. No data exist of the removal of any other locomotives from the railway.

30. On the 60cm gauge system, a train at Kuressaare station and depot in 1918.

Chapter 9
War of Independence and After

When the Germans withdrew from Estonia, the Red Army took the offensive from the east. The young Republic of Estonia was forced to build up a people's army at great speed, in order to defend the country's freedom and interests against an external enemy. The Estonian War of Independence began. Weapons and machines were needed for the front. A good source of their supply was the former Tallinn Naval Fortress. Some of its guns were sent to the front-line and some installed on armoured trains. Also two American 2-6-0s passed into the service of the narrow-gauge armoured trains. A commandant for Naissaar was appointed on 12 November 1918 by the new power. Arriving on the island on 16 November with a company of 38 men, he immediately started to restore some of the batteries. Some of the cannon in the old batteries had survived, while others had been damaged. By the beginning of December a 106.7 mm battery was ready for action, so it was designated as No 1. But because of the tense situation at the Russian front, two cannon were dispatched from there to the front near Tartu. Battery No 3 was formed on the basis of the remaining two cannon, but also that was short-lived - in May 1919 the cannon were sent to the front near Petseri. The railway lines had escaped destruction and were extensively used. For example, food from the kitchen and bakery in Pôhjaküla was sent by railway inspection car to battery No 4 in Lôunaküla. On 17 November 1918 an Estonian commandant was also appointed for the island of Aegna. On an inspection of the island it appeared that the German-built north shore battery with two cannon was undamaged. Four Russian 6-in cannon of the old type had been installed on the southwest coast quite recently. None of these weapons, however, had any locks. After a while the locks of the 6-in guns were accidentally found, but not those of the 105-ers. A lot of ammunition had been dumped in the woods, and shells had been brought out onto the pier to be shipped away. The first job the Estonians undertook was bringing four old 190-pood cannon and installing them on the western coast. Soon, however, they were taken to the front. The railway had not suffered, the locomotives and wagons were in good working order and were made ample use of during the restoration work.

After the War of Independence

Hostilities were over soon and on 2 February 1920 a peace treaty was signed in Tartu between the Republic of Estonia and Soviet Russia. Life in the former naval fortress returned to its daily routine. First the men began to dismantle the coastguard batteries on the West-Estonian islands which were no longer needed. The good cannon were taken to Naissaar, Aegna, Suurupi and Viimsi peninsula. All batteries on Saaremaa (Sôrve, etc.) and Muhu (Vôi) were dismantled. Dismantling of batteries started also on Hiiumaa (Hirmuste, Lehtma and Tahkuna). The dismantling of the Tahkuna cannon began in 1920. The work was carried out by men of the Tallinn Ship Repair Yard. The railway was kept functioning till the battery was fully dismantled in the late autumn of 1920. On 19 September 1920 fuel was procured for one more locomotive which took part in the dismantling, transporting the parts to Lehtma Harbour. The other locomotive stood idle. When the batteries had been dismantled, it was also decided to dismantle the locos and ship them out. One of them was sold to the Järvakandi glass works where it was kept in service as engine No 1 till the late 1940s. Also the other loco was sold but unfortunately nothing is known about the buyer, except that in the days of World War II it ended up in Romania where it worked till the late 1970s under the designation 763.226. The good cannon dismantled on Vormsi island were sent to Tallinn, while the engine was sold to the railway built about the same time to connect Jägala power station and cardboard mill with Raasiku Station on the Tallinn - Tapa broad-gauge railway. The Paljassaare battery in Tallinn remained untouched by the war but was dismantled. The concrete shelters there were taken into use as warehouses. One of the locomotives was sold to the Jägala cardboard mill, while the other one remained at the service of the warehouses.

31. Aegna pier in November 1918, on the day that a commandant appointed by the Estonian government arrived on the island.

32. Train carrying mechanics and transportation workers on Aegna island in 1918.

33. Dismantling of a 12-in gun at Tahkuna in 1920. Ammunition transporter wagons were positioned below for shells to be hoisted directly into the gun magazine.

34. Track dismantling inland on Saaremaa island in 1922.

35. The 60cm gauge railways continued in operation after the Germans' departure from Saaremaa. A well filled train behind a 'Feldbahn' 0-8-0T is seen here bound for Roomassaare in 1924.

36. A mixed train at Kuressaare station in 1924.

End of the Feldbahn Railways

The 600 mm field railway the German occupation authorities had built on Saaremaa was also on the verge of destruction. Although the Germans had drawn up a contract with the Kuressaare municipal government, the Ministry of Communications said the contract was fictitious and regarded the railway as its property. It was the ministry who made preparations to putting the Kuressaare-Orissaare line into working order and had even taken a loan for that purpose, but could not use it because of disagreement with the Kuressaare municipal government. In November 1922 dismantling of railway lines in the interior of the island was begun. The rails and fastenings were sold to Tartu businessmen and the Loksa brickworks, the seller being the Kuressaare municipal government. The branch from Roomassaare to Kuressaare and the mud transportation line from Suurlaht Bay was kept in operation quite a long time, however. A number of reorganisations were carried out on the railway. First, part of the useless track in the locomotive depot, the Roomassaare Port and the Castle Park was taken up. Wooden sleepers were replaced by metal ones along the whole track. Also the station was moved to a new site at 6 Allee Street where a new house was built for that purpose in 1924. The depot where all the rolling stock could be taken to shelter, retained its function as the main station. The Germans had given the town the priority right to use and buy the rolling stock. However, arguing that the contract was fictitious, the Ministry of Communications regarded the rolling stock on Saaremaa railways as its property. As it only brought the state a lot of conflict, it was interested in liquidating its share of the legacy as soon as possible. First of all the rolling stock, estimated at 1,150,000 sents, was yielded on credit to the Kuressaare municipal government for use on the Roomassaare-Kuressaare railway. In autumn 1928 7 steam, 1 diesel locomotive, 68 flat wagons and other equipment was sold to the Eesti Marmor shareholders' company which used them in quarrying on Jaagurahu island. The last items of the redundant rolling stock were sold as scrap to Danzig in 1929. The rolling stock of the Kuressaare-Roomassaare line was kept in a locomotive depot. It consisted of two wooden sheds. One, with a heatable stone workshop and two pits to facilitate repair work, held the locomotives in operation, while the other shed was used to keep the engines no longer fit for service, as well as other material which could come in handy as spare parts, or later, be sold. Two 'Feldbahn' engines, Nos 1509 and 1674, were kept running, while the diesel made up the reserve. The steam locomotives ran on the line till October 1940 when it was finally closed.

Reorganisation of the Tallinn Fortress Railway

When the naval fortress railway system around Tallinn lost its importance, reorganisation was also started there. The young Republic's army no longer had any use for such a large railway network and in 1920 it was handed over (formally at first) to the Republic of Estonia Railways Department. Most of the railways were no longer needed and their dismantling started in the same year. By 1921 64 km, and by 1922 31 km of main lines remained in service. The final handover of the railway by the Ministry of War to the Railways Department also occurred in that year. Civilian traffic was launched on the Tallinn-Vääna line. For a few years it was possible to ride even from Harku to Alliku or from Vääna to Humala, but then the lines were closed, though they did remain in the army reserve till the late 1930s. According to some data track on the Humala line was still there in 1944 after World War II had passed over Estonia, but was then taken up to to obtain rails to repair the narrow-gauge lines damaged in the war.

Changes in the Rolling Stock

From 1920 onward the former Tallinn Naval Fortress railway had two masters - the Ministry of War on the one hand and the Republic of Estonia Railways Department on the other hand. All locomotives kept at the Nômme locomotive depot, as well as those which had taken part in the building of the Paide-Tamsalu narrow-gauge line were registered in the Railway Department's books. Only the locomotives on the West-Estonian islands and those on the island of Naissaar were not included in the register. The Aegna engines, however, were for some reason entered in the inventory, as were those of Paljassaare and Männiku. On the basis of the inventory the strength of the fortress railway turned out to be the following:

37. A train at Roomassaare harbour in 1925.

38. Passenger train service on the fortress railways: a train arrives from Vääna at Nômme-Väike in 1920.

Type of locomotive	Number	Type of locomotive	Number
French M series	16	Koppel small 0-6-0 tank	5
Russian N series	6	Borsig 0-6-0 tank	1
American A series	12	Koppel small 0-4-0 tank	8
O & K K series 0-10-0	5	Baldwin 2-8-2 tank	1
Krauss 0-8-0	3	Cooke-Alco W series 0-6-0 universal	3
Koppel large 0-6-0 tank	5		

As of 1 June 1920 one Koppel 0-4-0 tank locomotive from Paljassaare had been sold, so 7 such locos remained. By the beginning of 1921 the number of locomotives on the books was 64. Early in that year one Kolomna 0-6-0-type steam locomotive (No 19) was sold to the Jägala-Raasiku cardboard mill railway, and another (unidentified) to the Fuels Central Committee which, it seems, put it into operation on the Lavasaare peat railway. Two French M series locos (one of them No 113) were sold to the Kohtla oil shale works where they were numbered 17 and 18. Locomotives Nos W 1 and W 2 were written off, scrapped, and W 3 was sold to the Kiviôli oil shale mine. Their tenders were not sold, however, and were later used with Koppel 0-6-0 tanks. By the middle of 1921 only 57 locomotives were registered in the Nômme depot books. As most tank locomotives lacked a serial designation, the railways department decided to put the matter right. All the tank locomotives still on hand in 1921 were given the serial designation T. Thus the Baldwin 2-8-2 became T 101, the big Koppel 0-6-0s were designated as T 105 - 109, Borsig's 0-6-0 as T 112 and the small Koppel small 0-4-0s as T 116 - 122. The numbers 1 - 12 of the American 2-6-0 A series locomotives were changed to 60 - 71, because otherwise they would have coincided with the numbers of the former Supplies Railway Society A series locomotives which had been received as spoils of war and had been entered in the Nômme depot books. In 1922 two Koppel 0-10-0 heavy locos were sold to Latvia on the basis of a convention drawn up upon the solution of the Estonian-Latvian border dispute. There K 1 was designated as Sp 779 and K 34 as Sp 778. Also Krauss T 104 was sold to an industrial enterprise (5173/C3). Later that locomotive turned up in Poland where it worked on the state railways under the designation Tx3 - 1278. This reduced the number of the former fortress railway locomotives at Nômme to 54. Some of them were rented to the military, some to industrial enterprises. T 109 and 118 worked on Aegna Island and T 117 at the Paljassaar magazines. One Koppel 0-4-0 - it has not been possible to establish which - also served at the Männiku military plant (magazine). In 1925 T 105, 106, 108, M 31, 34, 38, 42, 43 and N 57 were despatched to the building of the Sonda-Mustvee railway.

39. Former fortress locomotives N19 and a O&K T class 0-4-0WT in service at the Kohtla oil shale works in 1930.

40. A former naval fortress class M locomotive in service at the Kohtla oil shale works in 1930.

41. Former naval fortress locomotive K3, reclassified Latvian Sp 778, on shed at Valmiera, Latvia in 1924.

Chapter 10
Nationalisation of the Narrow-Gauge Railways

In 1926 a major change took place on the Estonian narrow-gauge railways, namely the state and private (Tallinn-Pärnu) narrow-gauge railways all over Estonia were united with the Republic of Estonia Railways. This caused major changes also in the locomotives' serial designation which was systematised with a view to an integral picture. Locomotives T 117 and 118 escaped redesignation. They worked on autonomous railways and were left at the disposal of the Ministry of War, as the state railways didn't have a use for them. The Aegna locomotive T 109 which was currently under repairs at Nõmme, received a new number, Rt 234. Also the Männiku locomotive received a new designation. The other designations were as follows:

Baldwin T 101	Ot 220
Krauss T 102 and 103	Nt 210, 211
Koppel T 105 - 109	Rt 230 - 234
Borsig T 112	Rt 237
Koppel T 110, 111, 113 - 115	Rt 235, 236, 238 - 240
Koppel T 116, 119 - 122	St 250 - 254
Koppel K 2	K 2
K 4	K 1
K 5	K 3
Kolomna N 55-57, 148	L 140 - 143
Russian field railway locos M31 - 40, 42, 43, 46, 98,	H 120 - 133
American A 60 - 71	G 100 - 111

As locomotives were badly needed on Aegna and at Männiku, they were rented to the military. Rt 234 was dispatched to Aegna where it was designated as the commandant's office locomotive No 2. One or two locos of the St series were also rented for service at the Männiku magazine.

13. Tallinn-Väike—Liiva—Nõmme-Väike -Vääna. Kitsaroopaline.

By the 1920's the fortress railways around Tallinn had largely outlived their military usefulness but some sections saw new life as 'common carriers', as part of the Republic of Estonia Railways extensive 75cm gauge network. This timetable dates from 1930.

11. Tallinn-Väike—Liiva–Nõmme-Väike -Vääna.

⚒19¹) 3.		†25²) 3.		21 3.		Km	Jaamad		⚒22¹) 3.		†26²) 3.		24 3.	
tul.	min.	tul.	min.	tul.	min.				tul.	min.	tul.	min.	tul.	min.
⚒	4 20	†	7 20	—	16 10	0	♦ Tallinn V.	↑	7 53	⚒	10 26	—	19 26	
4 30	4 31	7 30	7 31	16 20	16 21	3	Liiva		7 43	7 44	10 16	10 17	19 16	19 17
4 47	5 05	7 47	7 55	16 37	16 50	7	↓ Nõmme V.	♦	7 15	7 27	9 50	10 00	18 45	19 00
—	4 40	—	7 27	—	16 23	0	♦ Tallinn laiar.	↑	7 44	—	11 47	—	19 10	—
4 58	—	7 50	—	16 45	—	9	↓ Hiiu laiar.	♦	—	7 24	—	10 59	—	18 42
4 47	5 05	7 47	7 55	16 37	16 50	7	♦ Nõmme V.	↑	7 15	7 27	9 50	10 00	18 45	19 00
5 18	5 19	8 07	8 08	17 02	17 03	13	Harku		7 02	7 03	9 37	9 38	18 32	18 35
5 26	5 27	8 13	8 14	17 08	17 09	15	Rannam.		6 56	6 57	9 31	9 32	18 26	18 27
5 40	5 42	8 25	8 26	17 20	17 21	20	Sõrve		6 44	6 45	9 19	9 20	18 14	18 15
5 50	5 51	8 32	8 33	17 27	17 28	22	Vatsla		6 37	6 38	9 12	9 13	18 07	18 08
6 00	⚒	8 40	†	17 35	—	25	↓ Vääna ♀	♦	⚒	6 30	—	9 05	—	18 00

1) Rong nr. 19 ja 22 käigus äripäevadel. 2) Rong nr. 25 ja 26 käigus pühapäevadel ja pühadel.

This timetable dates from the winter of 1934/35 and shows a reduction to two return services per day.

42. Naissaar O&K 0-6-0WT No 3 on shed in 1935.

Republic of Estonia Naval Fortress and Its Railways

The Republic of Estonia Naval Fortress was made up of batteries on Naissaar and Aegna, as well as at Suurupi and Viimsi. Of the latter two only Suurupi had a railway connection. Major reorganisations took place on Naissaar. New batteries were built instead of the old ones which had been blown up. The 6-in cannon which had survived on the West-Estonian islands were brought away and installed there. Most former batteries were dismantled. Also 14.2 km of now redundant track was taken up, which brought the total length of the island's railways (with sidings) down to 23.5 km. An independent Naissaar commandant's office was set up. As for the locomotives on the island, they were designated as Nos 3 and 4, to fit into the

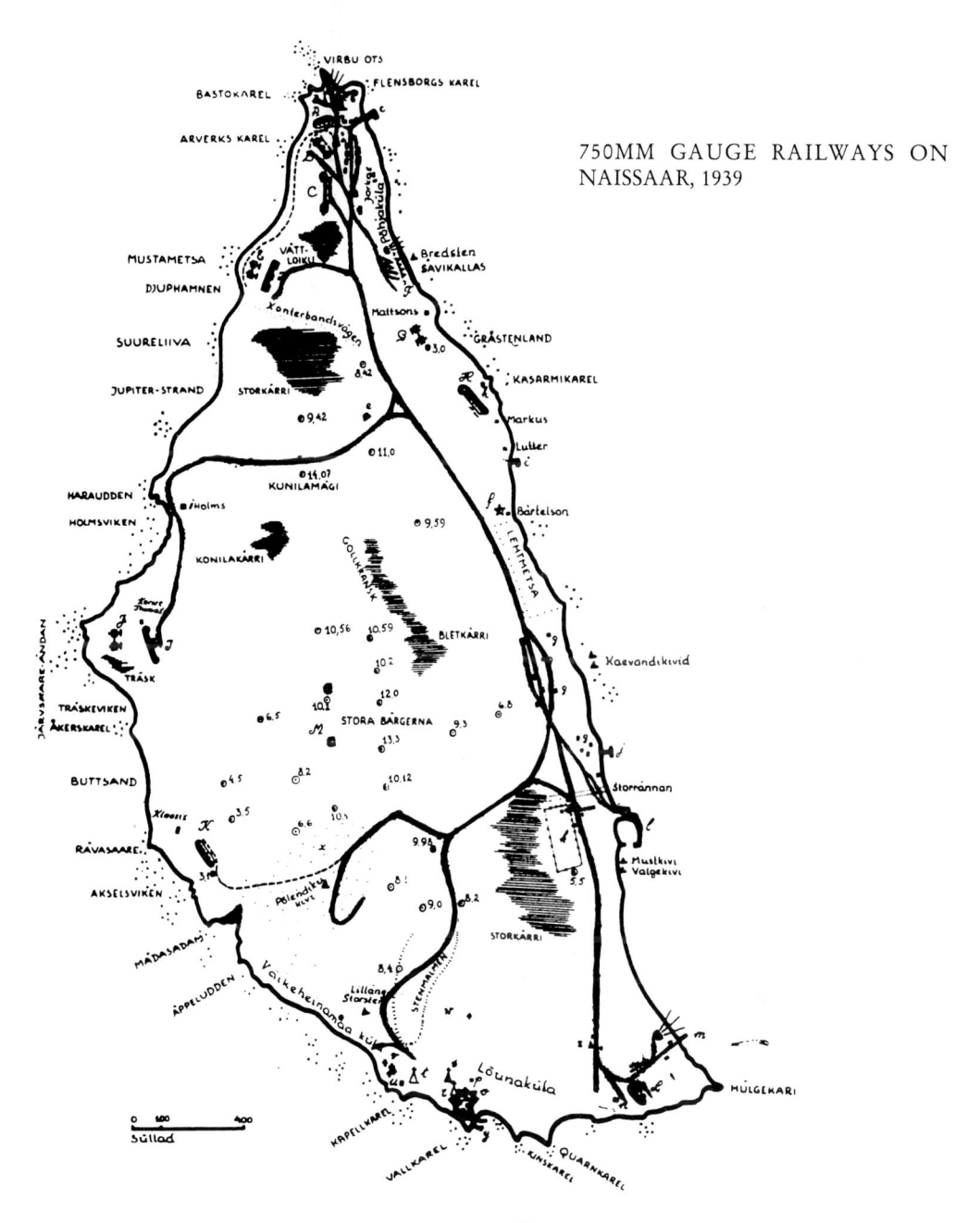

750MM GAUGE RAILWAYS ON NAISSAAR, 1939

43. Naissaar Tampella 0-6-2T No 4 depicted in 1938.

44. A train on Naissaar island in 1939.

unified pattern of the Bay of Tallinn fortifications system. No. 3 was a Koppel 0-6-0 tank locomotive and No 4 a Tampella 0-6-2T. On Aegna the reorganisations were of a slightly different nature. Restoration of battery No 15, now designated as No 1, was begun in 1919, with test shots fired from the easternmost armoured turret on 1 May 1919. The other turret was restored somewhat later. Also battery No 14, the new No 3, was restored in 1919. Battery No 2 was formed on the basis of the German battery. All the three batteries also needed a railway connection. So whereas on Naissaar the railway contracted, on Aegna it was extended by 5.2 km. In addition to the railway, a fire station and a railway repair shop were built on the island. Also Aegna received a separate commandant's office.

The Aegna locomotives were designated as Nos 1 and 2, they were a Koppel 0-4-0T (T 118) and a Koppel 0-6-0 (T 109) respectively. The way the island's locomotives were used can be characterised by the following figures dating from 1925: Aegna's No 1 was kept under steam for 2,745 hrs, of which 2,198 hrs was running time, the total distance covered being 8,250 km. As for Aegna's locomotive No 2, it was kept under steam for 966 hrs, of which running time was 831 hrs, while the total distance covered was

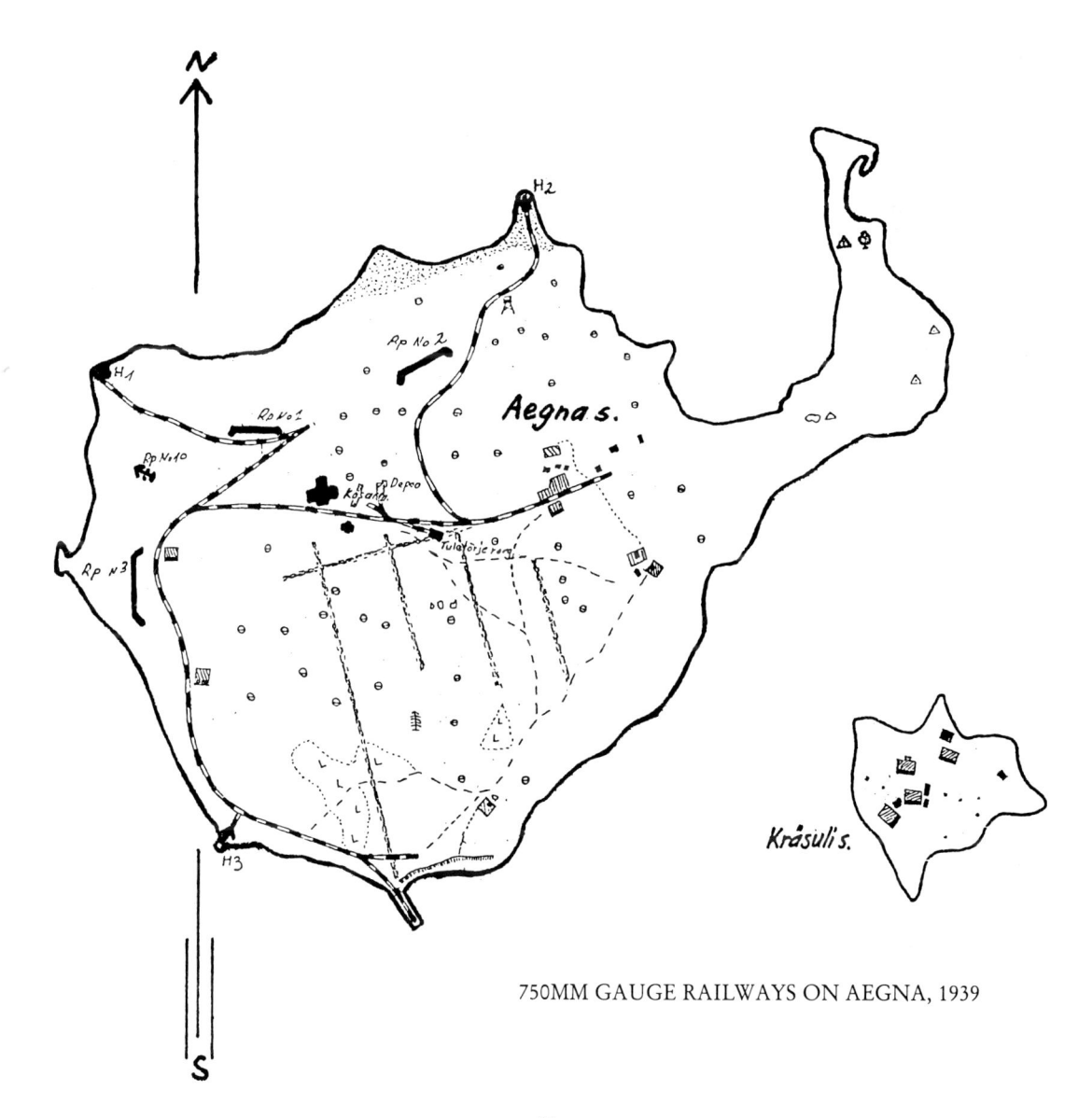

750MM GAUGE RAILWAYS ON AEGNA, 1939

45. The Aegna island fire fighting brigade in December 1927.

46. Aegna island locomotives Nos 2 and 1 on a shed siding.

3,120 km. On the basis of these figures we can conclude that No 1 was mostly used in maintenance work and in the fire train, while No 2 could not have been used much, for it was soon taken to the mainland to be repaired, and received a new designation there in 1926. Naissaar's No 3 was under steam for 3,315 hrs, of which 1,564 hours was running time, and the total distance covered was 7,805 km. Locomotive No 4 was kept under steam for 3,475 hrs, of which running time was 3,113 hrs and the total distance covered 6,566 km. Here we can conclude that while No 3 was running errands to the batteries in the various parts of the islands, making for more distance covered in fewer hours in service, No 4 maintained both passenger and freight traffic between the main port and Pôhjaküla. Also several railway inspection cars were in use on the island. One of them, fitted with a water-cooled engine, was built in the commandant's office workshop in 1929. As a rule, the most urgent business on the island was done by inspection car. The Paljassaare system belonged to the area of the Tallinn commandant. The locomotive there obviously didn't have a special designation, but bore the former number T 117. It was used for the transportation of military supplies from magazine to pier from where they were taken by ship to the coastal defence batteries. Suurupi battery had no locomotives allocated to it and rented locomotives were used there over a certain period of time.

By 1923 the technical conditions of the Sôrve-Suurupi railway became so poor that it became unsafe for locomotive traffic. The line remained practically idle and at the mercy of the elements. It was used once in 1924 for the transportation of cannon to Suurupi, the wagons being pushed by soldiers. The line was taken up in 1925. However, an autonomous line a couple of kilometres in length between the two batteries and the depots remained in service on the Suurupi coast. Transport on it was by horse and trolley. Aegna, Naissaar and Suurupi, among other places, have been mentioned in the secret protocol of 17 June 1940 about the stationing of Red Army troops on Estonian territory. It is known, however, that those places were occupied on the early morning of the day that the protocol was signed. The coastal defence batteries were handed over to the Red Army by a document dated 12 June 1940, long before Estonia was proclaimed a Soviet republic. This was occupation in practice.

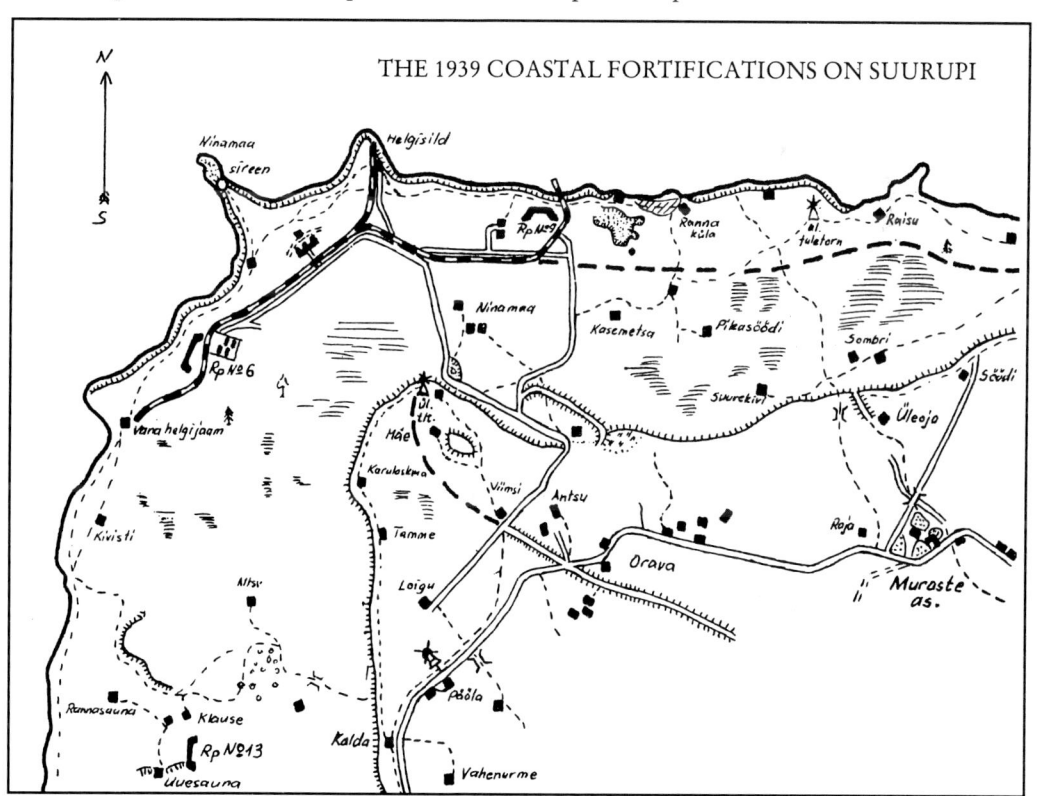

THE 1939 COASTAL FORTIFICATIONS ON SUURUPI

47. Former naval fortress O&K 0-6-0WT Rt235 in 1935.

48. Former naval fortress Krauss 0-8-0T No Nt211 in 1938.

Chapter 11
Later History of the Fortress Locomotives

In the early 1930s the Republic of Estonia Railways gradually began to sell locomotives which stood idle or were less economical. Among the first all St series locomotives were written off the books in 1931. Some were sold to the army (those that had been rented to it), some stood in the depot until 1935 when they were cut up for scrap. In 1938 the Baldwin Ot 220 and Borsig Rt 237 were written off and cut up into scrap. In the same year the Koppel Rt 238 (No 7191/14) was sold to the Lavassaare peat works where it was designated as RT 1. It worked there until 1966 and was then scrapped. By the beginning of 1940 more locomotives had been written off: Rt 232, 233, 234, 235, 236 and 239, the Kolomna locomotives L 140, 142 and 143, as well as the French-built locos H 120, 122, 124, 125, 126, 128, 129 and 132. The Koppel Rt 231 was for some reason redesignated as Rt 233 and Rt 240 as Rt 231. The Kolomna L 141 was rebuilt as a tank locomotive, whereupon it received the designation Lt 140. The Koppel Rt 234 stayed on Aegna island, so is not found in any of the 1939 lists. The boilers of Rt 235 and 239 were installed as central heating boilers in the old Tallinn electric trains depot, and were replaced only in 1955. The boiler of Ot 220 was installed in the Tallinn-Kopli locomotive depot. It was damaged in the 9 March 1944 Soviet air raid and was later replaced by another one.

In the middle 1930s a decision was taken to modernise the K series 0-10-0 locos by converting them from saturated to superheated steam. For that purpose superheaters were built into their boilers at the Estonian State Railways Main Plant in Tallinn, along with new cylinders. No other changes were made. The power of the engines increased considerably, though not their running speed. The locomotives were designated by a new series, Kk, whereas the enumeration remained unchanged. By the beginning of the 1930s the Cooke Works G series 2-6-0s had also come to the end of their lives. Their boilers started

49. Former naval fortress Baldwin 2-8-2T No Ot220 in 1935.

50. Former naval fortress Alco 2-6-0 No G108 in 1926.

51. Former naval fortress Kolomna 0-6-0 No L140 in 1929.

to fail one by one, and it was no longer possible to repair them. So it was decided to build new boilers. The question immediately arose where drawings for the boilers were to be obtained. Fortunately there were men among the veterans at the Môisaküla railway plant who could make new drawings from the old boilers. Using these drawings the building of new boilers began at the State Railways Main Plant in Tallinn, the rest of the rebuilding being done at Môisaküla. At the same time new cabs and six wheeled tenders were built for the engines. So the locos G 100, 101, 105, 106, 107, 108, 109 and 111 received new boilers and a new appearance. In 1938 it was decided to modernise the G series locomotives once again by transferring them from saturated to superheated steam. For that purpose an old locomotive was cannibalised. The old frame, wheels and some other parts were used in the building of a new loco which received a totally new boiler, cylinders, cab and tender. The locomotives were designated by the series Gk, but the enumeration was not changed. Gk 103 was the first locomotive to be completed in the summer of 1939. It performed so well during its test run from Tallinn to Vääna that the Railways Department bosses were soon forced to forget their initial reluctance and give full credit to the new design. In 1940 Gk 110 and in 1941 Gk 102 and 104 were built. That same year also G 106, 109 and 111 were stripped for rebuilding, but the plan was never effected because of the war. The dismantled parts were shipped to the Soviet hinterland where they became raw material for the war industry.

52. Former naval fortress O&K 0-10-0 No K1 (ex K4) in 1932.

53. Former naval fortress M class 0-6-0 No H124 in 1929.

54. A class Kk 0-10-0 locomotive in 1938.

55. The first Gk class locomotive undergoing trials in 1939.

Chapter 12
The Railways under German Occupation (1941-44)

In summer 1941 Estonia was once again occupied by the Germans. Retreating, the Soviets tried to take with them anything they could. So the locomotives Kk 1, 2, 3, G 100, 105, Gk 110, H 121, 123 and 130 were taken to Russia. The locomotives Rt 230, 231, 233, 234 (on Aegna), H 127, 131, 133, Nt 140, G 101, 107, 108 (at Sonda), Gk 102, 103 (at Sonda) and 104 remained at the disposal of the German occupation army. In 1942 the Germans brought to Estonia Sp 778 (K 3) which had earlier been used on the Tallinn Naval Fortress railway. It was not put into operation, however, but stood in the old locomotive depot in Tallinn which was later also used as a wagon shed. Because of a lack of locomotives on the Sonda-Mustvee line G 107, then also 101 and 108, and later Gk 102 and 103 were taken there. The Gks didn't stay long at Sonda, for in 1942 the so-called Ruijena express was put into operation, and all the Gk series locomotives were transferred there. The Russians left Naissaar in a hurry, without any destruction or evacuation of property. German air raids on the island obviously contributed to their hasty departure. Only the commandant remained, promising to blow up all the most important structures. That never happened. Instead he waited for the arrival of the Germans and then gave himself up as prisoner. Also the railway and the locomotives survived. They were used by the occupation authorities till summer 1944. On Aegna, however, the Russians managed to blow up all the batteries. The railway remained in working order, as did both the locomotives. A temporary German battery was set up on the island, and the railway and its rolling stock were also put into use.

The Germans' Departure from Estonia

In 1944, immediately before their departure from Tallinn, the German military authorities brought away locomotive No 4 from Naissaar and locos Nos 1 and 2 from Aegna. The Naissaar loco was given a new designation, Ot 240, and it worked on Estonian railways till it was dismantled in 1953. The Aegna locomotive No 2 was designated as Rt 234, and it also worked in Estonia until 1955, after which it was dismantled. The Aegna locomotive No 1, however, was loaded on a lorry and taken to an unknown destination. During the war the locos Rt 230 and 231 (ex 240), G 107, Gk 103, H 127 and Lt 140 disappeared without a trace. A large number of Estonia's narrow-gauge locos were taken by the Germans to Puikule Station in Latvia where they were blown up. Among those locomotives were Nt 210 and 211, as well as H 133. Nt 211 was restored by the Latvians and in 1951 sold to Siberia where it was put into operation on a logging railway. The other locomotives were written off. Also the Koppel Rt 233 (ex 231) and Gk 104 were driven by the Germans to Latvia. They were arbitrarily appropriated by the Latvians, without informing the Estonian Railways directors. Both locomotives worked in Latvia until August 1952 when they were dismantled.

56. A 1944 view of the Nômme locomotive depot, showing damage caused by the German air raid of 1941 (see page 61).

57. Alco 2-6-0 G102, as rebuilt in 1941, at the head of a train of war booty coaches standing at Sôrve station in 1947.

58. Alco 2-6-0 No G101 at Môisaküla in 1957.

Chapter 13
The Railways under Soviet Control

When Soviet forces entered Tallinn, they ordered an overhaul of Sp 778 (K 3) to be carried out within one twenty-four hour shift, at the point of submachine guns. In the course of the overhaul, intended to restore the original rating of the locomotive, its designation was also changed to K 778. After a short test run it took off with an ammunition train for Virtsu. H 131 worked at Môisaküla until 1949, and was then dismantled. G 101 worked at various Estonian narrow-gauge railways locomotive depots until February 1958 and then remained waiting for its last hour to strike. G 108 remained at the Sonda depot and worked on the Mustvee line, also until 1958. Then the loco was dismantled, but its boiler was installed at the Viru-Nigula bakery as a central heating boiler. Gk 102 ran on the Tallinn-Vääna line until February 1954. However, as Soviet Russia desparately needed non-ferrous metals, orders were given to dismantle the engine without delay, because its firebox and superheater pipes were made of copper. In 1945 the former Koppel 0-10-0 Kk 1 returned from Russia and was put into service on the Tallinn-Türi line, pulling heavy-weight freight trains. In 1956-1957 the locomotive was used to provide steam for the central heating system of the Tallin-Väike depot. Then the locomotive was dismantled and the boiler was installed in the stationary boiler-house of the depot, to be later replaced by the boiler of a broad-gauge Su locomotive. Immediately after the end of hostilities the Naissaar locomotive No 3 was brought for repairs to Môisaküla. It was the very first locomotive to have been repaired at Môisaküla after the war. In the course of repairs it received the designation PT 3 (RT 3) in Cyrillic, and was returned to Naissaar. It worked there into the 1950s when it was replaced by 1930s Russian-built 0-8-0 type 159 series locomotives. There is one more very interesting fact which deserves attention. Namely, in 1946 the Finnish Äänenkoski woodpulp mill bought from the military of the Kirkkomaa island fortress railway a small O&K 0-6-0T (No 7194/14) which had formerly belonged to the Estonian Naval Fortress railways. The loco had been taken to Kirkkomaa either during World War I by the Russian army on strategic considerations, or had been sold or given to the Finns by the Republic of Estonia government in 1920. The locomotive had earlier served either on Muhu island or at Nômme, and worked on the Äänenkoski-Suolahti railway until 1964. Today it stands on display as a museum piece on the territory of the old Äänenkoski mill.

The Later Fate of the Estonian Fortress Railway

The fate of the Nômme locomotive depot has been remarkable. Up to 1941 it was used by the army as an ammunition depot. In a German air raid on Tallinn in August 1941 the Nômme depot was hit by a bomb. It started a stupenduous pyrotechnical display, the detonations going on almost non-stop for twenty-four hours. Wagon wheels and pieces flew through the air like insects, they could be found at the distance of several kilometres from the depot. Only the walls remained. After the war what had remained of the building was taken into use as a depot: a roof was built, and the swing bridge pit was filled in. It continues in this function also today. Also the girder of the fortress railway bridge across the Pirita River at Iru found a use. It was used to restore the Reiu River bridge on the Lelle-Pärnu railway in 1944. The only fortress railway line kept in operation was that from Liiva to Vääna. Up to 1957 it was serviced by steam locomotives, not an infrequent sight in Estonia in those days.

The first locomotives put into service on the line in 1944 were the Henschel/Krenau German 'Feldbahn' locos HF 11001 and 11009, brought from the Blue Hills area near Narva where the Germans had built a Feldbahn network during the years of the Nazi occupation. A little later some Romanian-built 764 series 0-8-0 steam locomotives were added to the German ones. They ran on the line till 1957 when diesel traction took over. Also in use on the Vääna line were some Gr series 0-8-0 steam locos built in 1947-1951 at the former O&K factory in Germany as war reparation, as well as KV 4 series 0-8-0 lightweight locomotives built at the Hungarian MAVAG works in the 1950s. Also, the steam engine Gk 102 was in service on the line. The coaches were trophies brought back from Germany. From 1958, locomotives of the TU2 series built in 1957-1959 in Kaluga, Russia, as well as timber-frame coaches made

59. O&K 0-10-0 Kk1, as rebuilt in the 1930's, at Tallinn-Väike shed in 1957.

60. Former naval fortress locomotive O&K 7194/14 standing as a mounted exhibit outside the Äänenkoski woodpulp mill in Finland.

61. A class 764 0-8-0T, a type supplied by Schwatzkopf and Resita.

62. A class Gr locomotive built in Germany in 1947 as part of war reparations.

63. A class Kv4 locomotive built in the 1950's in Hungary.

64. Train with TU2-262 locomotive at Rahumäe station in 1969.

at Môisaküla in the 1930s began to run on the line. The line was quite popular with the passengers, but like the whole narrow-gauge railways system, it was a thorn in the flesh of the Railways Administration's new Russian bosses. A plan to close down the line was devised, but it had to be justified somehow, because of the large number of passengers. So they set out to reduce it articificially. The trains were made to run at unsuitable times - late at night and very early in the morning. Naturally it did the trick, providing the justification for closing down the line - for lack of passengers - in 1962. The part of the line from Liiva to Nômme remained in service, however, because of the Hiiu grain silo which had a link to the narrow-gauge railway. The stretch stayed in service until 1971 when the Tallinn narrow-gauge railway terminal was closed down.

The Russian military authorites seem to have been even more conservative about the dismantling of the narrow-gauge railway. The Männiku magazines continued to be used until the late 1970s. A MUG 2 series railway inspection motor car built 1937 in Russia was kept in service there. Its remains were extant in 1989. In 1985 it became known that a fully preserved system of depots and fortress railways existed and was being actively used at Paljassaare in Tallinn. The line passed right through the shallow lake which had formed between what had formerly been the island and the mainland. It had even been modernised by the occupation army who had built a new branch to it. Obviously they never thought they would have to start pulling out soon. Thanks to *perestroika* the situation began to gradually change, and Estonians were once again granted greater freedom of movement in their own country. That particular railway had four TU6A series locomotives (built 1955-1961 at Kambarka), of which one was in constant use. Mainly 14-tonne flat wagons were used. There were also two covered freight vans rebuilt from flat wagons (both extant today). Traffic on the railway was more or less regular until 1987 when, as a consequence of the building of the Tallinn waste water purification plant, outflow from the lake was obstructed. The water level started to rise rapidly and the railway was flooded. The military tried to save the situation by cutting a number of drainage canals but that did not suffice. So both the railway and the rolling stock are standing idle. There are hopes that after the occupation army have left the line will be turned into a museum.

In 1986 and 1992 it became possible to make a tour of Naissaar, fully held by the Soviet, later Russian, military. It came as a major surprise that nearly 15 km of serviceable track and about 7 km of non-serviceable track of the railway dating to the years of the pre-war independence has been preserved. In 1986 there were three TU6A series locomotives on the island. TU6A-1904 was kept in operation, while the others were used as a source of spare parts. Exploring the near history of the island it emerged that after the steam engines four MD54-4 railway inspection motor cars built at the Istyinsk engineering works in Russia had been brought to the island. The first such car arrived in 1969, and the other three in the early 1970s. Only their wrecked frames were sighted at the time of the first visit. The steam locos had disappeared without a trace, and none of the servicemen were able to provide any information about them. There are only flat wagons on the island, most of them built in 1952-1959 at the Tchesnokovka engineering works in the Altai region of Russia. There are also some new 14-tonne ones from the Demikhovo wagon works in Orekhovo-Zuyevo. A small ship crane had been installed on one 1952-built flat wagon. Due to poor maintenance and sheer neglect it was no longer serviceable.

The track on the island is of varied stock: the rails from Lôunaküla to the port are 19 kgs per metre, of the type made in England in 1927. The line to the port, the western branch and a few kilometres of the line to the north of the island are built of 22 kgs per metre Krupp rails dating from 1893-1901. This branch also has some modern Russian rails made by the KMK works and weighing 24 kgs per metre. Quite well preserved imported timber sleepers lie under the English rails. Elsewhere timber sleepers from a still earlier time have been alternately replaced by 1960s concrete sleepers. Recently timber blocks have been wedged under the rails. In 1986 a water-cooled railway inspection motor car was standing under an awning in Pôhjaküla, probably the one made on the island in 1929. A more modern car, recently repaired, stood in a shed beside the lighthouse, guarded by a vicious dog. In summer 1992 the old car was nowhere to be seen, and only the frame and wheels had survived of the new one. Also the vicious dog was

65. Two TU6A diesels marshall a goods train at Lôunaküla on the island of Naissaar in 1992.

66. Improvised tender at Lôunaküla, Naissaar, 1992.

67. Naissaar scene - abandoned wreck of MD54-4 diesel loco, August 1992.

gone. The impressions from the last visit to the island were depressing: most of the branch leading north had been wrecked by the wheels of a large cross-country truck, very well characterising the nature of the occupation army. Rubbish and wreckage could be seen all around. One of the greatest relics of local military history is facing destruction.

68. Diesel TU6A 1754 at Paljassaare in 1992.

69. Old wagon at Paljassaare in 1992.

70. Track on Naissaar pier in August 1992.

71. Train loaded with scrap inland on Naissaar island, August 1992.

Chapter 14
Relics of the Naval Fortress Railways

Concrete structures of the former coast defence batteries are still visible on the islands of Saaremaa, Hiiumaaa, Muhu and Vormsi. The more experienced visitor will also discern the railway embankments. The fortress structures of the Tallinn land front are all extant, and can be found in various places around and in Tallinn. In many places also railway embankments can be seen, some of them have been taken into use as motorways. In Tallinn itself we can still see gun emplacement pits at Nõmme, depots in the Sütiste tee area at Mustamäe and railway embankments in their neighbourhood. Also at Pääsküla there are some surviving gun emplacements, a stretch of railway embankment and a railway bridge. A narrow-gauge flyover at Rahumäe, the pillars of a bridge over the Prita River at Iru, as well as a railway bridge at Vääna have all come down to our days. Of station buildings those of Vääna, Sõrve, Suurupi, Harku, Nõmme-Väike, Rahumäe, Liiva, Pääsküla, Alliku and Tammemäe, as well as a pointsman's cabin between Männiku and Saku have survived. Besides there are water towers at Sõrve and Liiva, the roundhouse at Nõmme and many magazine and warehouse buildings in and around Tallinn. Visitors to Aegna island may see the ruins of the concrete batteries and the command post, as well as the railway embankment, partly with the rotting sleepers still visible in the ground. The old locomotive depot was used up to the 1970 to keep firewood, but has now been demolished. The barracks building is used as a canteen where holidaymakers can have a modest meal. There is much more to see on Naissaar than on Aegna. However, in February 1993 access to the island was still only by special permission of the occupation army. Hopefully also that part of Estonia will soon be liberated from foreign troops and be turned into a pleasant recreation area for the people and visitors of Tallinn. The island's old railway could be used for recreational purposes.

72. Command post of the 12-in gun battery on Naissaar island in 1992.

73. Vääna station, presently serving as a post office. The location of the station name plate can be distinguished by the bare patch over the front door.

74. Sõrve water tower, still standing in 1992 (compare with illus.11).

Bibliography

1. H. Gustavson. Merekindlused Eestis 1913-1940 (Naval fortresses in Estonia 1913-1940) (manuscript).
2. V. Gussarova, O. Karma, G. Lukin. 100 aastat Eesti Raudteed (100 years of Estonian Railways). Eesti Raamat, Tallinn 1970.
3. Estonian State Archives, section 49, list 1, record 3034, pp. 8, 50, 102, 140; section 498, list 12, record 20, pp. 56, 58, 70.
4. Estonian Railway Administration Archives.
5. Estonian Railway Museum Archives.
6. Kuressaare Municipal Archives. E. Püüa. Saaremaa raudteedest (About Saaremaa Railways).
7. Personal archives of P. Klaus, Vice-President of the Estonian Museum Railway Society.
8. A. Jämsen. Äänenkosken-Suolahden Yksityisrautatie (Äänen-koski-Suolahti private railway). Museorautatieyhdistys ry 1984, pp. 64, 109.
9. W. A. Rakow. Russische und sowjetische Dampflokomotive (Russian and Soviet steam locomotives). Transpress 1986, pp. 315, 326.
10. A. B. Gottwaldt. Heeres Feldbahnen (Army field railways), pp. 27, 28, 29.
11. R. Bude. K. Fricke, Dr. M. Murray. O. & K. Dampflokomotiven. Lieferverzeichnis 1892-1945 (O. & K. steam locomotives. Delivery list). Railroadiana Verlag 1978.

Appendix 1

Orenstein & Koppel Locomotives Delivered to the Naval Fortress Railways in Estonia in 1913-1914

Class	Works No	Year	Power	Remarks
0-4-0	6780	Nov. 1913	45 HP	Aegna loco No 1 (T118)
0-6-0	6884	Jan. 1914	90 HP	Tahkuna loco
0-6-0	6885	Jan. 1914	90 HP	Tahkuna, later CFR 763.226
0-6-0	7191	Mar 1914	50 HP	Rt 238, later RT 1 at Lavass.
0-6-0	7192	Mar 1914	50 HP	
0-6-0	7193	Mar 1914	50 HP	
0-6-0	7194	Mar 1914	50 HP	1946 to Äänenkoski works
0-6-0	7195	Apr 1914	50 HP	
0-6-0	7196	Apr 1914	50 HP	
0-6-0	7197	Apr 1914	50 HP	
0-6-0	7198	Apr 1914	50 HP	
0-10-0	7205	May 1914	325 HP	K 1, Sp 779
0-10-0	7206	May 1914	325 HP	K 2, Kk 2
0-10-0	7207	June 1914	325 HP	K 3, Sp 778, K 778
0-10-0	7208	June 1914	325 HP	K 4, K 1, Kk 1
0-10-0	7209	June 1914	325 HP	K 5, K 3, Kk 3
0-4-0	7503	June 1914	45 HP	Tallinn, State ammunition works
0-6-0	7841	June 1914	90 HP	On Môntu-Sôrve line
0-6-0	7842	June 1914	90 HP	Naissaar loco No 3
0-6-0	7843	July 1914	90 HP	Aegna loco No 2
0-6-0	7844	July 1914	90 HP	
0-6-0	7845	July 1914	90 HP	
0-6-0	7846	July 1914	90 HP	

Compiled from O & K's catalogue

Appendix 2
French-built Russian Field Railway M Series Locomotives
Fulfilment of Russian Ministry of War Order

Company	Place	Works No.	Year	Serial No
La Corpet	Paris	No 1057...1060	1905	M 1...4
Denain	Cail	No 2669...2708	1905	M 3...44
Five-Lilles	Lille	No 3299...3326	1905	M 45...72
France-Belge	Reims	No 1516...1543	1906	M 73...100
Batignolles	Paris	No 1574...1587	1906	M 101...114

M Series Locomotives in Estonia

Designation	Company	Year	Works No
M 31 (H 120)	Denain	1905	2695
M 32 (H 121)	Denain	1905	2696
M 33 (H 122)	Denain	1905	2697
M 34 (H 123)	Denain	1905	2698
M 35 (H 124)	Denain	1905	2699
M 36 (H 125)	Denain	1905	2700
M 37 (H 126)	Denain	1905	2701
M 38 (H 127)	Denain	1905	2702
M 39 (H 128)	Denain	1905	2703
M 40 (H 129)	Denain	1905	2704
M 42 (H 130)	Denain	1905	2706
M 43 (H 131)	Denain	1905	2707
M 46 (H 132)	Five Lilles	1905	3300
M 98 (H 133)	France-Belge	1906	1541
M 113 (No 17)	Batignolles	1906	1586
M ? (No 18)	?	?	?

75. A works official view of No.M100, built by Franco-Belge in 1906. Locomotives of this type ended up in Tallinn.
(collection - Keith Taylorson)

Appendix 3
Russian 86 Series Field Railway Steam Locomotives

The locos were ordered in 1902 by the Main Administration of Engineers Troops in 1902 from the Kolomna Engineering Works where their building started in 1903. The first consignment was completed in 1905. The locomotives were classed into the I series and were designated by the numbers 1 to 39. In 1916 the 86 was taken into serial production, with small modifications. It also received a new serial designation, N. The first consignment of such locomotives, N 1 - N 402, was completed in 1916-1917. A new consignment was built in 1929-1930, but unfortunately their number is not known. Locomotives of the 86 (N) series worked on the Peter the Great Naval Fortress Railway in Estonia, but also elsewhere in the country. In 1916 when the Fuels Central Committee was organising the haulage of timber from the woods, a 7-8 km stretch of logging railway was built at Sonda. There were four N series locomotives on the line, two of them designated as N 141 and N 143. In 1922 the locomotives temporarily passed into the subordinance of the Railways Administration that had bought the logging railway. In 1925 the locos returned to the former owner who put them to work at the Kohtla oil shale mine where they stayed in service until 1944. Another N series locomotive, N 340, came to Estonia as booty in the Estonian War of Independence in 1919. It was handed over in 1920 to the Estonian State Railways, which sold it some time later to the Lavasaare peat works, along with another locomotive of the same type from the Nômme depot.

Appendix 4
German 'Feldbahn' Locomotives in Estonia

Running Nos.	Builder	Year	Works Nos.
894...910	Vulcan	1916	3214...3230
911...920	Henschel	1916	14674...14683
964...968	Maffei	1916	4762...4766
969...970	Schwartzkopff	1917	6150...6151
971...975	Schwartzkopff	1917	6265...6269
976...990	Borsig	1917	9839...9853
991...1000	Henschel	1916	14921...14930
1071..1118	Henschel	1918	15948..15995
1141..1200			
1201...1245	Henschel	1917	14931...14975
1271...1273	Humboldt	1917	9318...9320
1287..1288	Jung	1917	2554...2555
1289..1290	Hohenzollern	1917	3701...3702
1291...1320	Jung	1917	2628...2657
1321...1410	Borsig	1917	9900...9989
1441...1455	Hanomag	1917	8280...8294
1486...1545	Henschel	1917	15225...15284
1546..1551	Henschel	1917	15306..15311
1552...1569	Maffei	1917	4830...4847
1570..1601	Krauss, Manchen	1917	7344...7375
1623..1630	Esslingen	1917	3817...3824
1631..1700	O & K	1917	8331...8400
1701..1720	Linke-Hoffmann	1917	1501...1520
1794..1805	Hanomag	1918	8301...8312
1900..1925	Borsig	1918	10292..10317
1977..2004	Schwartzkopff	1918	6715...6742
2516..2539	Hartmann	1918	4160...4183

750mm GAUGE LOCOMOTIVES - TABLE OF PRINCIPAL DIMENSIONS

Type	Max speed km/h	HP	Boiler heating surface sq.m.	Firebox grate surface sq.m.	Pressure kg/cm²	Cylinders diam mm	Cylinders stroke mm	Driving wheel diam mm	Weight
T112 0-6-0WT Borsig	25	40	25.7	0.45	12	210	300	625	12.9t
Gr LkM 0-8-0 O&K	35	250	42.9	1.6	13	800	400	800	39.8t
Kv4 0-8-0 MAVAG	35	175	37.1	1.0	13	285	300	600	28t
T105/9 0-6-0WT O&K	25	90	33.6	0.5	12	270	350	615	16t
T102/ 0-8-0T Krauss	4 25	100	32.6	0.7	12	275	300	690	18.9t
T101 2-8-2T Baldwin	25	100	51.4	0.65	12	275	300	760	20t
159 0-8-0TT Russian	25	100	32.1	0.7	13	285	300	600	22t
764 0-8-0T Resita	30	150	50.0	0.95	12	320	400	800	24.2t
HF11001/9 0-6-0TT Henschel	30	110	34.4	0.7	13	300	350	700	29.5t
Gk102/10 2-6-0 Alco reb. Estonia	75	150	43.0	0.9	12	280	400	860	36.8t
M31/11 0-6-0 France	325	70	25.8	0.6	11	250	400	725	21.3t
N(86) 0-6-0 Kolomna	25	60	26.4	0.55	12	256	300	600	19t
W(B)1/3 0-6-0T Alco	30	-	49.4	0.9	11	279	406	774	8.45t
A60/71 2-6-0 Alco	40	90	39.4	0.9	11	280	400	860	18.4
No.4 0-6-2T Tampella	25	90	25.2	0.55	11	-	-	750	14.7t
K1/5 0-10-0 O&K	30	225	100	2.0	13	390	400	790	50.8t
(reb Kk)	30	350	88.4	2.0	13	390	400	790	49.4t
T116/22 0-4-0WT O&K	20	45	18.4	0.4	12	210	300	600	8.9t
T110/5 0-6-0T O&K	25	50	29.8	0.45	12	270	350	615	16.2t

T105 -T109 (Rt230-234) O&K 1914

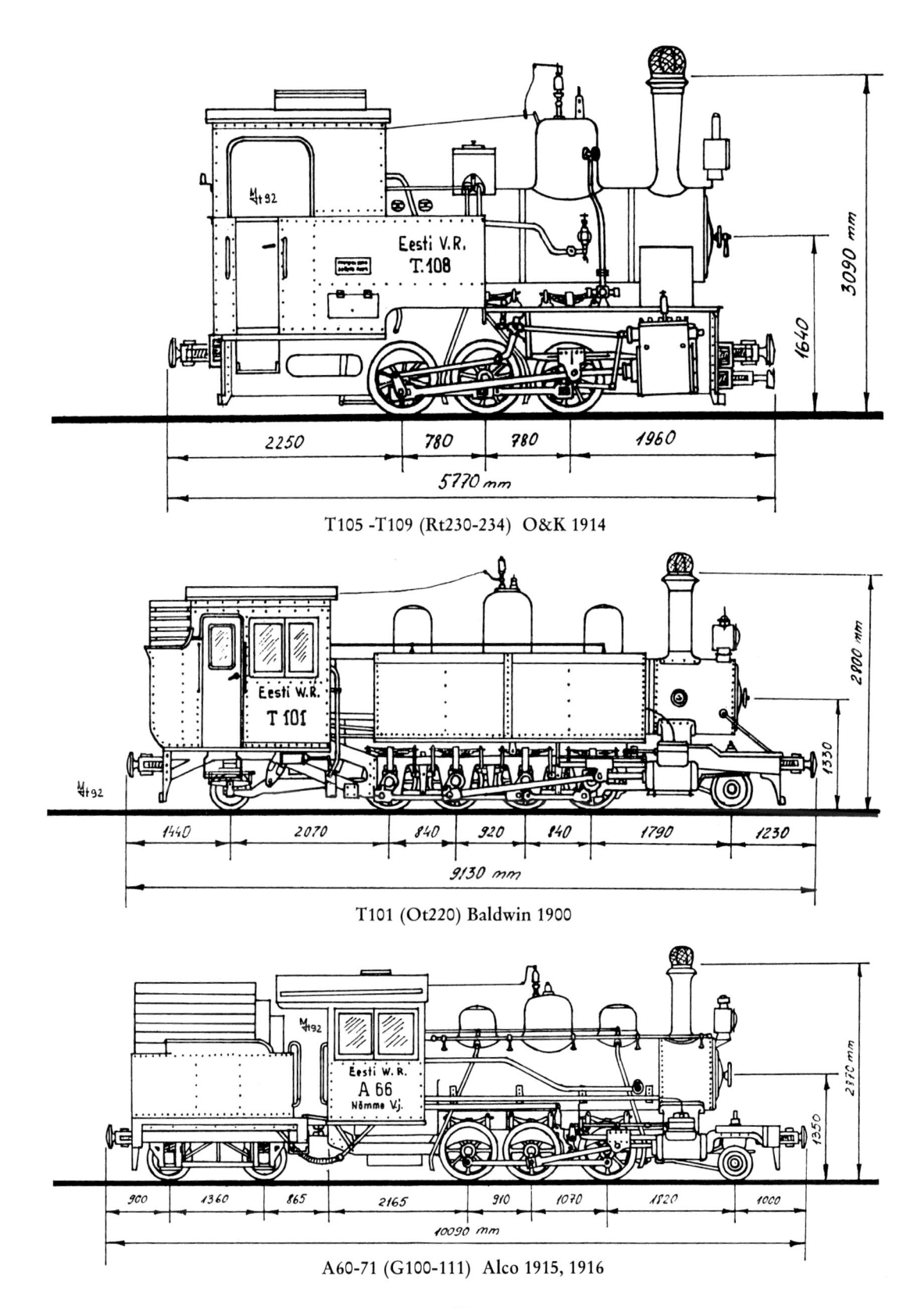

T101 (Ot220) Baldwin 1900

A60-71 (G100-111) Alco 1915, 1916

T112 (Rt237) Borsig 1914

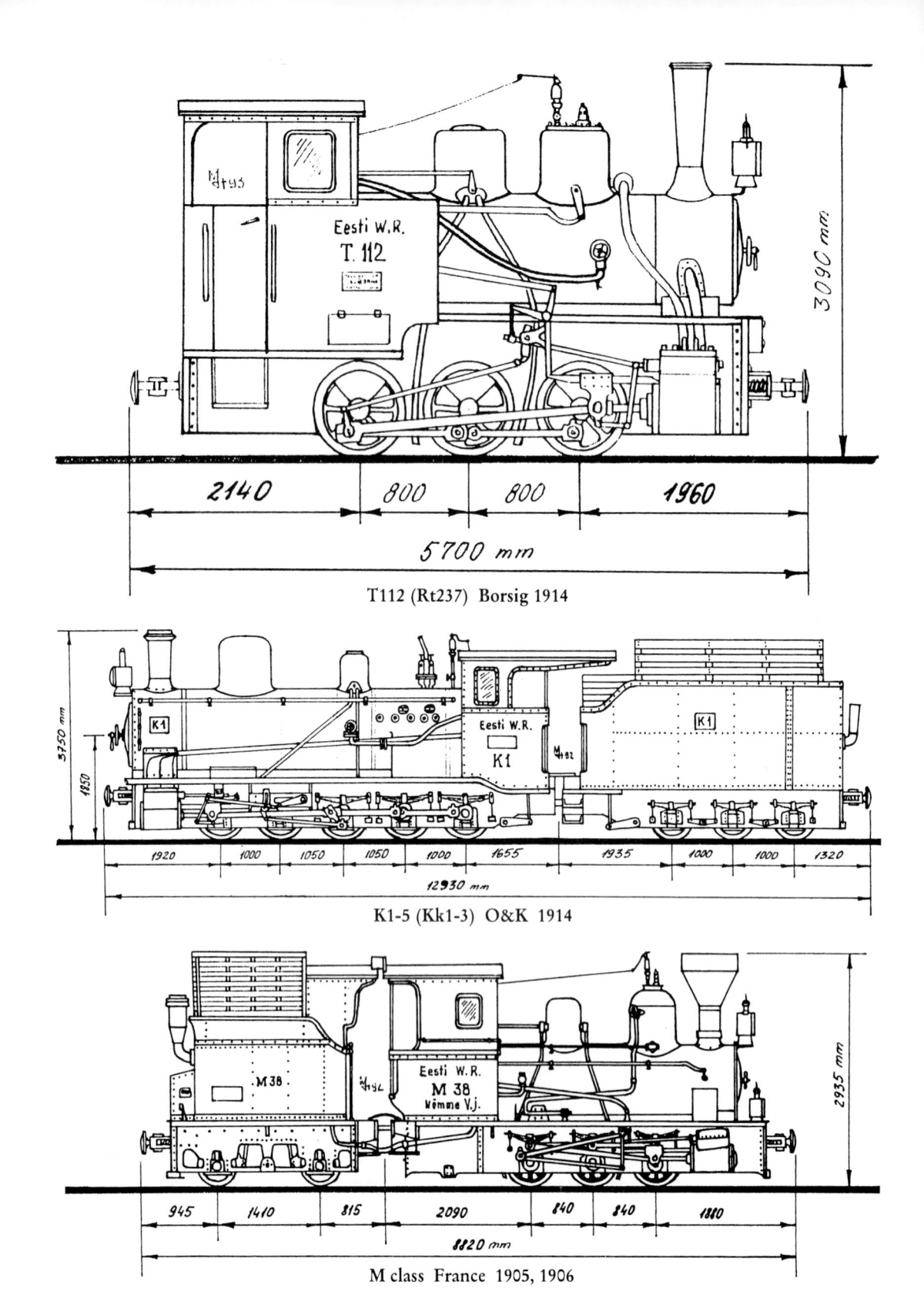

K1-5 (Kk1-3) O&K 1914

M class France 1905, 1906

T102-104 (Nt210,211) Krauss & Co. 1899....1909

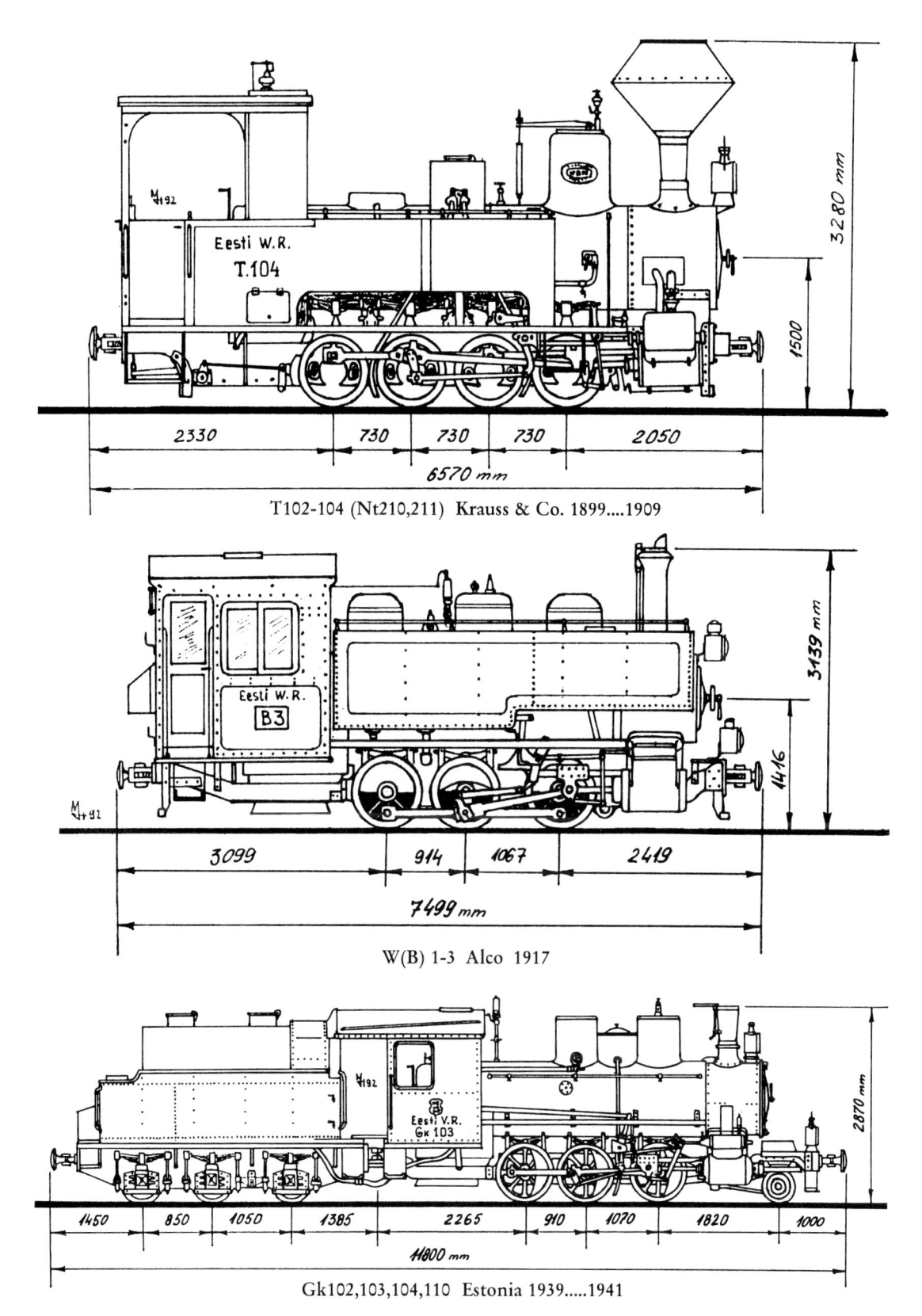

W(B) 1-3 Alco 1917

Gk102,103,104,110 Estonia 1939.....1941

No.4 (Ot240) Tampella 1907

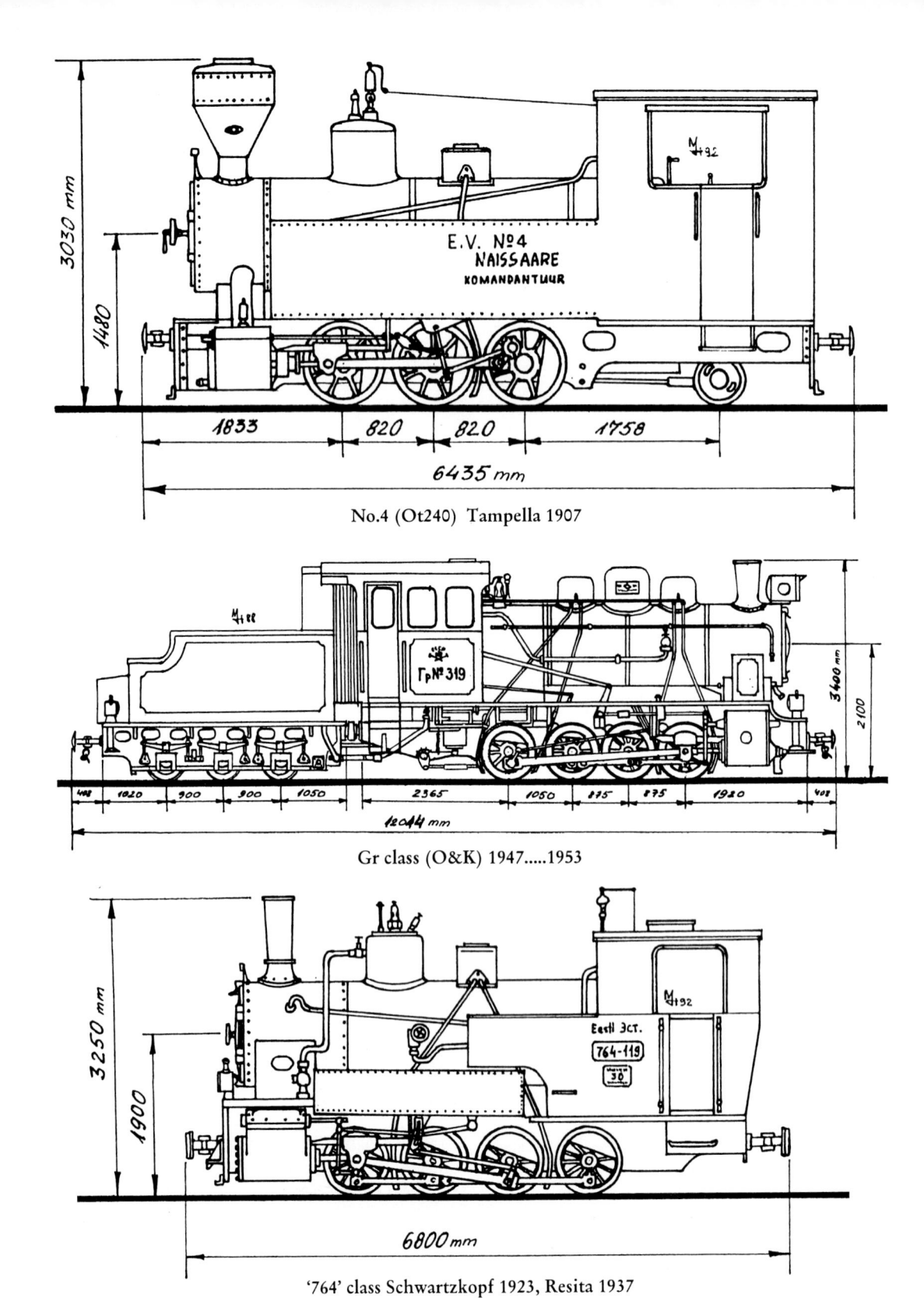

Gr class (O&K) 1947.....1953

'764' class Schwartzkopf 1923, Resita 1937

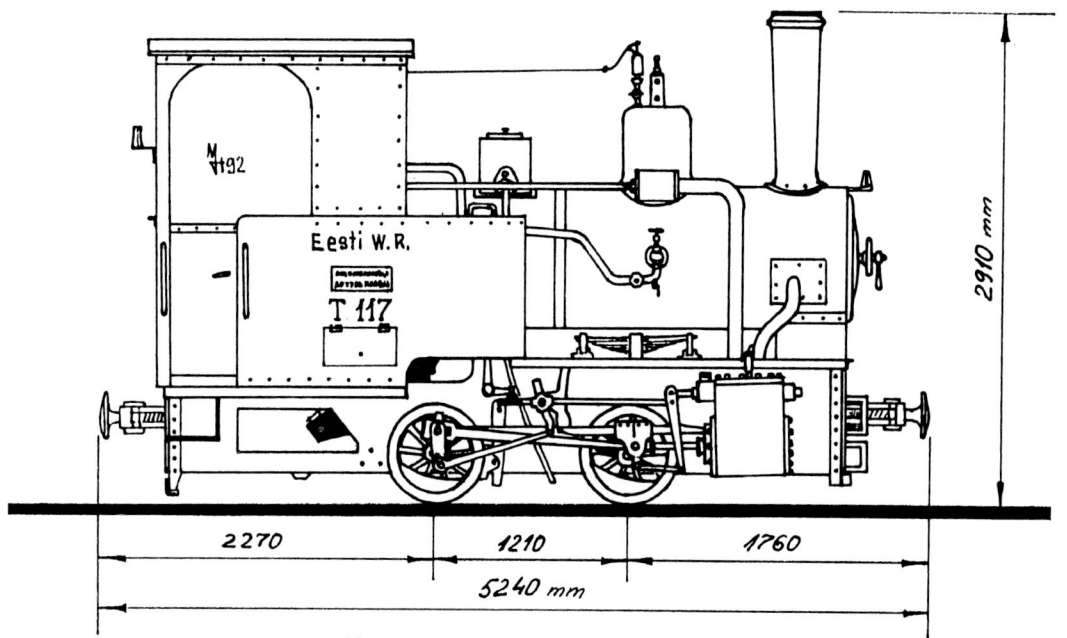

T116-122 (St250-254) O&K 1913, 1914

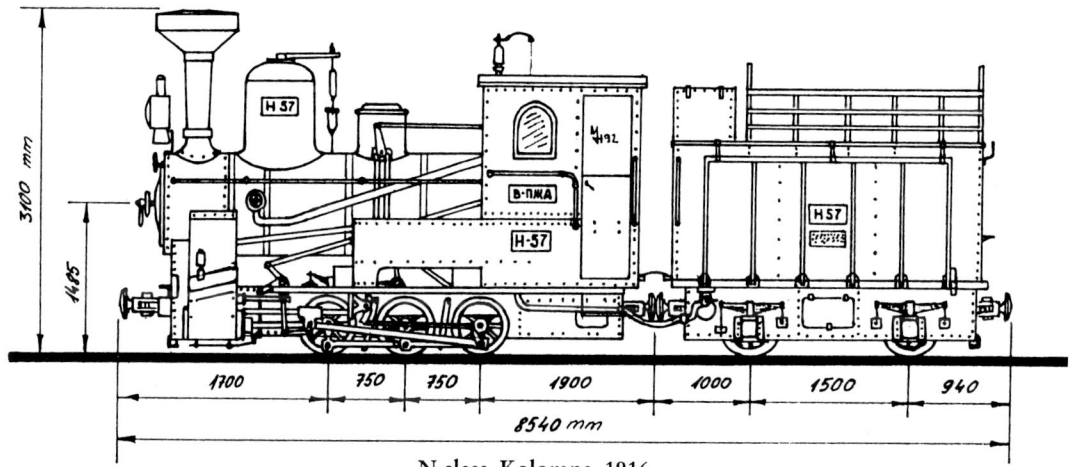

N class Kolomna 1916

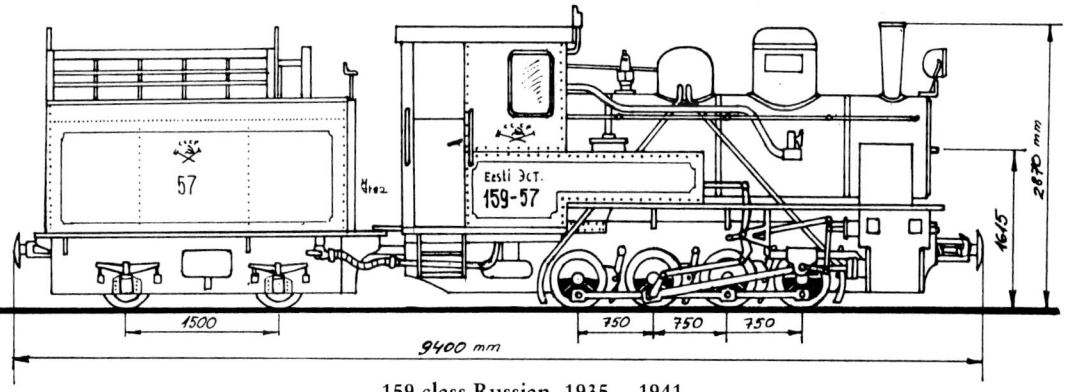

159 class Russian 1935.....1941

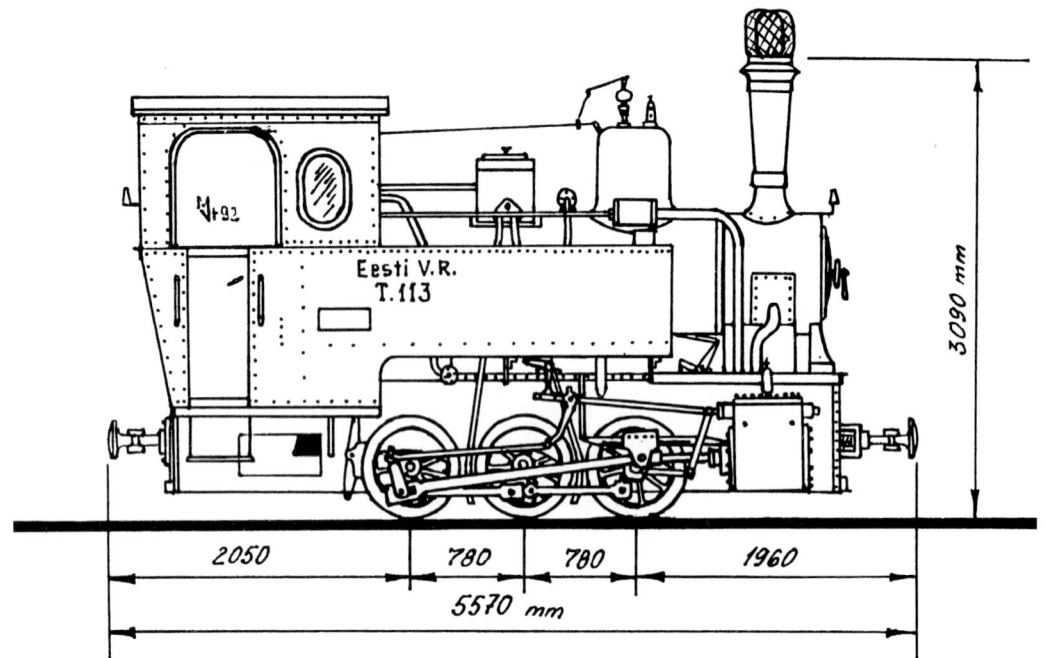

T110-115 (Rt235-240) O&K 1914

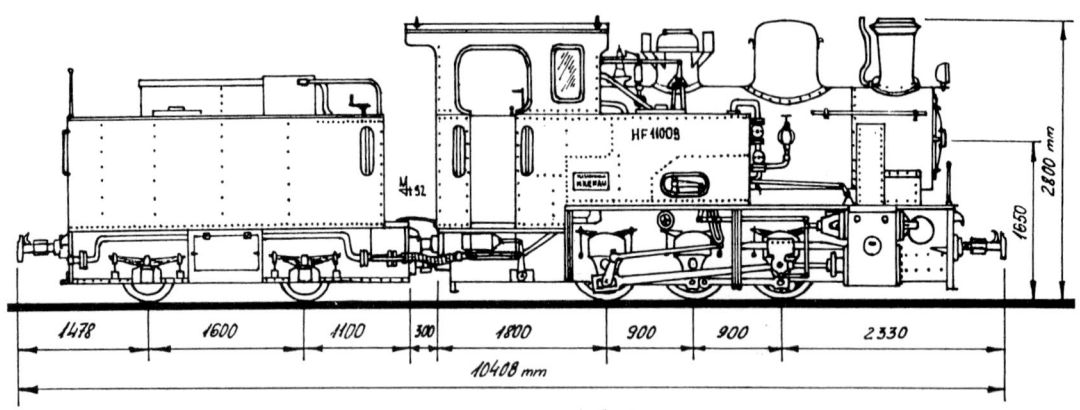

HF11001,11009 Henschel/Krenau 1941

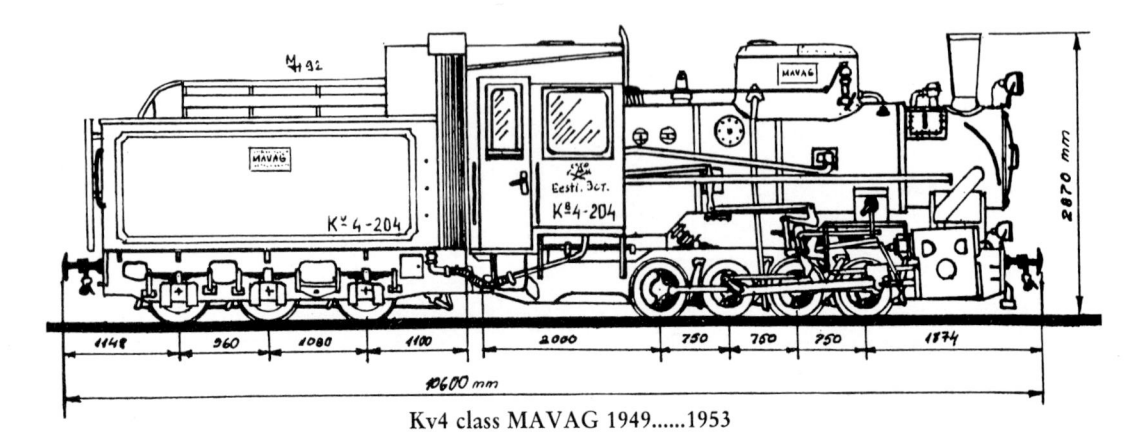

Kv4 class MAVAG 1949......1953

80